KU-754-036

In Praise of Benedict

Cardinal George Basil Hume, O.S.B.

HODDER AND STOUGHTON
LONDON SYDNEY AUCKLAND TORONTO

We are grateful to the Queens College, Oxford for permission to reproduce the cover illustration.

British Library Cataloguing in Publication Data

Hume, George Basil
  In praise of Benedict.
  1. Benedictines – History
  1 Title
  271'.1   BX3006.2

ISBN 0 340 26410 1

First published 1981. Copyright © 1981 by Cardinal George Basil Hume. All rights reserved. No part of this publication may be reproduced or transmitted in any form or by any means, electronic or mechanical, including photocopying, recording, or any information storage and retrieval system, without permission in writing from the publisher. Printed in Great Britain for Hodder and Stoughton Limited, Mill Road, Dunton Green, Sevenoaks, Kent by Richard Clay (The Chaucer Press) Ltd, Bungay, Suffolk.

In Praise of Benedict

Introduction

From 21 March, 1980, until 21 March, 1981, Benedictines throughout the world celebrated the 1500th anniversary of the birth of St Benedict. As the only Benedictine in the College of Cardinals, I was invited to be present for, and to speak at, many of these celebrations. The invitations which I was able to accept came from abbeys, priories and parishes in England, France, the United States of America and Italy. The talks at these functions were therefore delivered under very different circumstances and to very different audiences. All of them are concerned with St Benedict and his Rule.

The opening talk in this printed version, "The Monastic Ideal in Earthenware Vessels", was a lecture given to the American Cassinese Congregation at their General Chapter. It speaks of the monastic ideal being contained in imperfect people, the vessels or clay pots. All the other talks were addresses, sermons or homilies, given during celebration Masses. Sometimes the congregations were composed largely of monks and nuns who follow the Rule of St Benedict; at other Masses, the congregation was mostly lay people in Benedictine parishes; once I spoke to the assembled bishops of Europe. In every case it has been for me a labour of love, and an offering to St Benedict for this anniversary.

Taken together, the talks explore various aspects of St Benedict and his Rule and consider what message, if any, he may have for the men and women of our time, one thousand five hundred years later. The talks are prefaced by a brief life of St Benedict and some information about the Rule for those readers unfamiliar with "Benedictinism".

Contents

Preface

Apart from the approximate dates of his birth and his death we know comparatively little about the life of St Benedict. He was born about A.D. 480 and died about A.D. 547. His whole life was spent in Italy yet few individuals have had as profound an effect on the Western world.

He lived in a period of turmoil as a dying Empire gave way before the onslaught of the barbarian armies. Four years before St Benedict was born, the last of the Roman Emperors, the boy Romulus, was deposed by the chieftain Odoacer. The Hun, Attila, had come from Africa and had invaded and devastated the Italian peninsula in A.D. 451. Four years later the Vandal, Genseric, attacked Rome and laid it waste just as Alaric had done less than half a century before. During Benedict's lifetime barbarian chieftains ruled in the West even though the Roman Empire was technically under the Emperor of Byzantium. Benedict died during the time of the Gothic War which was an attempt by the Eastern Emperor, Justinian, to regain control of the former Roman Empire. Justinian's success was partial and temporary; the next wave of barbarian invaders, the Lombards, caused even more devastation than their predecessors. The Lombards sacked St Benedict's own monastery at Monte Cassino and forced the monks to disperse. This was probably in the year A.D. 581.

So the age in which St Benedict lived was one of conflict and violent change. In his lifetime the Italian peninsula knew alternating periods of war and peace. The wars, devastating the countryside and ruining crops, aggravated the grave economic problems of the dying Empire; there were serious shortages of food and, at times, real famine. Many must have felt as St Jerome did, when he wrote shortly after the sack of Rome in A.D. 410: "My voice is choked and sobs interrupt the words which I write; the city is captured which took captive the world." The Roman Empire was in its death throes; a new age was coming to birth. None of these events, or their significance, are recorded or alluded to in the Rule of St Benedict. The purpose of the Rule was something quite different. St Gregory the Great in his *Dialogues* does touch upon them, but only indirectly. In one passage he speaks of famine; in another he describes the visit of a barbarian chieftain, Totila, to the monastery of Monte Cassino. But from our vantage point we can see a fuller picture. We can understand first that St Benedict did not live in an untroubled period of history, and secondly that his influence on the new age which was emerging was very considerable and obviously of far greater significance than St Benedict himself could possibly have foreseen.

It is a simple matter to recount the recorded facts of his life. Most of what we know about him comes from St Gregory's *Dialogues*, Book Two of which details the "Life and miracles of St Benedict". St Gregory stresses the wonder-working rather than the more ordinary circumstances of the saint's life, but the broad outline of his life seems fairly certain.

As a young man, Benedict was a student in Rome. However, he found life there so decadent and corrupt that he abandoned his studies and went in search of God. He went to live alone in a cave at Subiaco where he lived as a hermit for three years. A monk named Romanus provided him with food.

After three years or so of solitary prayer and penance, Benedict's presence in the cave at Subiaco became known locally. A community of monks from Vicovaro invited him to be their Abbot, and after repeated invitations, he reluctantly accepted. His attempt to impose high standards on their way of life, however, provoked the hostility of some of them and they tried to kill him with poisoned wine. Their attempt failed, but their intention succeeded, for Benedict left them and returned to Subiaco.

In the Aniane valley and the surrounding countryside he gradually established twelve small communities of monks. His growing reputation for holiness, however, aroused the jealousy of a nearby priest, Florentius. He eventually sent Benedict a poisoned loaf of bread. Once again, the saint did not consume the poisoned food, but this and other attacks made on his monks decided Benedict to leave Subiaco. So, about the year A.D. 529, he founded the monastery of Monte Cassino within the walls of an ancient fortress on the summit of the mountain.

It was while he was Abbot of the monastery of Monte Cassino, that Saint Benedict drew up his monastic rule.

Although, strictly speaking, his Rule was not an innovation, St Benedict is justly called the "Father of Western Monasticism" because it has had such profound effects on religious life in Europe and throughout the world. Benedict drew upon pre-existing monastic rules in writing his own Rule, but he modified much of these as a result of his own experience, of his own understanding of men, and of his own searching for God. The result, "a beginner's rule" as he described it, is a document which combines detailed practical rules for living in community with pages of sublime spirituality. But this is to draw a false distinction because all of it, even the most disciplinary sections, is suffused with spirituality, is firmly rooted in Scripture and is motivated by faith.

And all this is the work of a lay man – for St Benedict was not a priest and was not writing for priests. Most of the early monks were not ordained. It was the pastoral work they undertook with the faithful that over the cen-

turies gradually led to the present situation in which most
monks are ordained priests. This does not seem to have
been envisaged by St Benedict. Hence, his Rule was written to help groups of Christians to unite in their search
for God, and to support and encourage each other in so
doing, to be a "school of the Lord's service". He saw the
monastery as a self-sufficient, self-supporting unit under
the spiritual and paternal care of its Abbot. Each house,
within the limits of the Rule, was to establish its own programme of monastic training; each was seen as a "family"
to which the monk vowed stability and to which he be-
longed for the rest of his life.

In the family of the monastery, three activities were pur-
sued: prayer, spiritual reading and work. All three were
seen by St Benedict as ways of serving God; but pride
of place – "to which no other work is to be preferred" –
went to the daily praise of God, the public singing of the
Prayer of the Church. This *par excellence* was the *opus
Dei*, the work of God, to be performed faithfully, whatever particular individuals might be feeling. The prayerful
reading of the Scriptures and of spiritual writers was intended to lead to private prayer and to prepare the heart for
the public praise of God. Work, initially probably manual
work in kitchen garden or in some employment to serve
the other monks, expanded to include intellectual work,
writing of books, the copying of books, illustrating manuscripts, music, art, education – in a word, the development
of all the skills and arts needed for the monastery, its
liturgy, its administration and its pastoral work.

St Benedict's monks took, and still do to this day, three
vows. The vow of stability is principally to a specific
monastic community. The monk belongs to a particular
family; loyalty to it and involvement in its life is an important means both of the formation of the monk and of
support to him, as he pursues with his brethren his search
for God. The vow of conversion of manners – more diffi-

cult to explain – means, in effect, that the monk commits himself to live as a celibate and to renounce personal ownership. The vow commits him to adopt the kind of virtues which are normally and traditionally associated with the monastic life, and to go on trying throughout his life to become better and more wholehearted in his service of God. The third vow, obedience, has important negative qualities: it saves the monk from becoming personally ambitious, self-willed and domineering; positively, it enables the monk to live more consciously as Jesus Christ lived, that is, as totally dedicated to the will of his heavenly Father. It is, in fact, a sign of the monk's love, and, just as important, it is a certain way of learning how to live in a loving way. It is perhaps an unfashionable attitude to our modern way of thinking, but it is my belief, anyway, that it leads to a greater inner freedom, and in fact can only truly be understood after some years of living by it. Obedience is an important virtue for St Benedict, and he insisted that obedience was not only to be shown to the Abbot, but the monks must be obedient to each other. This is one of the necessary conditions for life in a community. Obedience is closely related to the virtue of humility; St Benedict's teaching on this latter virtue is an important contribution to writing on the spiritual life. No monk can succeed in his monastic vocation unless he be a humble man.

Today there are just over ten thousand monks and nearly nine thousand nuns belonging to the Benedictine Confederation, and there are a great number of Benedictine Sisters, especially in the United States. But the Benedictine family also includes Cistercians, both the reformed Trappists and the "non-reformed", and there are many others who follow the Rule of St Benedict. It is a large family. A word must be said about Benedictine nuns and sisters. The nuns are enclosed and are strictly contemplative; the sisters, like many of the monks, are engaged in the active apostolate. All these must be mentioned, for not only do they, too, follow the Rule of St Benedict, but they have a special devotion to Benedict's sister, St Scholastica. We do not know a great deal about her, but St Benedict was clearly fond of her, and they saw something of each other. St Gregory records a touching incident when St Scholastica's prayers prevented her brother leaving her; she prayed and the ensuing storm achieved what her entreaties to him had failed to do. They were both originally buried in the same grave at Monte Cassino, until separated when, following the sacking of the monastery, their remains were, in all probability, taken to France.

St Benedict wrote his Rule for "cenobites", that is for those who live in monasteries, accepting a rule of life and the authority of an Abbot. The life of a hermit was clearly to be exceptional and was to be for those who were mature, both humanly and spiritually. In fact, those most likely to make good and successful hermits will be those who have known how to live well in community. St Benedict was particularly harsh when he wrote of two types of monks, of which he thoroughly disapproved. I refer to the "sarabaites" and the "gyrovagues". The former were those monks who "in their actions still conform to the standards of the world ... they live in twos and threes, or even singly without a shepherd ... their law is their own good pleasure; whatever they think of or choose to do, that they call holy; what they like not, that they regard as unlawful". The "gyrovagues" spend their whole lives wandering ... staying three days in one monastery and four in another, ever roaming and never stable ..." (Rule Chapter I).

In every monk, or at least in some, there lurks a potential "sarabaite". I for one have known the danger. But I did enjoy being a "gyrovague" during this year of celebration, accepting hospitality in several monasteries. To all my kind hosts on those occasions and to my own monastic brethren at Ampleforth who helped me to avoid becoming too much of a "sarabaite" in practice and whose company and spirit made the stability of the "cenobite" more attractive than the wanderings of the "gyrovague", I offer these few further thoughts on the "monastic thing".

Archabbey of St Vincent's, Latrobe, USA
9 June, 1980

I have been tempted to start this talk by protesting my inadequacy to be addressing you on so important an occasion, and in such august company. There is, I believe, something slightly vulgar and embarrassing about self-depreciation made in public. The temptation is nonetheless there, and I intend to succumb to it.

First, I am in no sense a scholar of any kind, and least of all of the Rule of St Benedict – but I do, incidentally, accept the priority of the "Rule of the Master", upon which St Benedict depended so much. Secondly, my experience of monastic life is very limited. I know one monastery well, in one Congregation, and great though my affection for it is, and although I believe it to be a great monastery, I would not claim that it is necessarily normative as far as the rest of the Benedictine world is concerned. Thirdly, I am speaking in the light of a monastic experience among monks. I do not forget the great number of our Benedictine Sisters, whether living in enclosure, or more actively involved in the apostolate. They follow the Rule of St Benedict as we do. There are many of them, and they play a vital part in the total life of the Benedictine family. But I cannot speak of them with any authority. And finally, I live in a different world now ...

So what have I got to offer you? "Thoughts recollected in tranquillity?" Hardly that, I confess. Memories of a peaceful life in a secluded cloister, away from life's problems, and with the mind focused, uninterruptedly, on eternal truths? Would that it had been so! There is no point in pretending to you that the outsider's view of the inside of the monastery corresponds always to the reality. We are not romantics. But neither must we be cynics. Our monastic ideal is a very noble one. St. Benedict's Rule puts before us a vision of what the monastic life might be, and indeed, can be. If we falter around the foothills – and it seems thus often – we must, nevertheless, keep our eyes on the summit of the mountain. Of course we are "earthenware vessels", frail and inadequate no doubt, but "let us ask God that He be pleased, where our nature is powerless, to give us the help of His grace" (Prologue).

What I am offering you then, are the personal reflections of a former Abbot, rather than a learned and scholarly analysis of the Rule. My subject is that the "monastic ideal" is contained in "earthenware vessels". Let me speak first about these latter.

I have often thought that the Rule was written for a monastery that functioned imperfectly. For instance, the Rule seems almost to assume that there will be misbehaviour in the Oratory (Ch 52), that there will be late arrivals for prayer and for meals (Ch 43) and that complaints will be made about the quality of the clothes (Ch 55). Furthermore, St Benedict never seems too happy with his officials, or at least he is well aware of how things can go wrong: the Prior, the deans, the cellarer, the priests and the craftsmen all have to be on their guard against being "puffed up with pride". There are, too, those passages which lay down how the delinquent monk is to be treated. No monastic legislator would include such draconian measures in Constitutions today, and get away with it. Again, there is the suggestion that St Benedict thought that the monks of his day compared very unfavourably with the monks of former generations. After all, monks in the past used to pray the whole Psalter each day (Ch 18); if monks cannot manage that now, at least let them make certain that they pray all the psalms in the course of one week. In the old days, monastic life was a continuous Lent

(Ch 49); it is not so in these days, but please do make a special effort when Lent comes. And if monks cannot keep off wine, as used to be the case, then let wine be drunk in moderation (Ch 40). There is something harsh about the use of words like "slothful" and "lukewarm" to describe this new generation of sixth-century monks. (Ch 18).

Do these passages suggest that the author of the Rule was too critical and unsympathetic, rather timorous and slightly suspicious, fearful of his officials and unwilling to impose the ancient disciplines? Was he, rather reluctantly, settling for lower standards? No, the author of the Rule was a realist. He knew that he was dealing with ordinary human beings, and so with imperfect people. He recognised that spiritual gifts and natural talents have been unevenly distributed, that in every monastery there is a great diversity of temperament and background. Concessions have to be made to the weak, but the strong must not be held back, except where *singularitas* might prove an even greater danger than human frailty. It sometimes does.

The two chapters on the Abbot, too, have something to say about the "earthenware vessels". Chapter two, for instance, instead of being entitled: "What sort of man should the Abbot be?" might equally well have been headed: "What sort of monks should the Abbot expect?" In listing the qualities with which the Abbot should be equipped, the Rule was anticipating the kind of problems which he would inevitably meet. Some of the monks will be "undisciplined and restless", others, "obedient, meek and patient". Some will be "negligent" and "rebellious". And what of those "bold, hard, proud and disobedient characters" who have to be checked by "the rod and corporal punishment?" ... Indeed, the Abbot, conscious of the "difficult and arduous task he has undertaken", has to know how "to rule souls", and so must "adapt himself to many dispositions". Is not that, perhaps, his main burden? To realise that every monk is different; to understand the problems of each one; to handle them with kindness, sympathy and firmness, and to recognise their frailty. All this makes great demands on the Abbot and calls for considerable reserves of patience and endurance. But how wrong the Abbot would be to approach his task with suspicion and fear. The Rule emphasises this point.

The Abbot, drawn as he is from the ranks of the brethren, is not allowed to forget that he, too, is one of the "earthenware vessels": "Let him always distrust his own frailty ..." He has to be at pains not to be "headstrong or anxious, extravagant or obstinate" (Ch 64). Perhaps one of the consolations in becoming Abbot is to realise, once the brethren begin to confide and entrust their weaknesses and fears to him, that his monks are like him – labouring under a sense of inadequacy.

Thus there emerges from the Rule the fundamental guiding principle for every Abbot to help him in the handling of those committed to his care: "Let him temper all things that the strong may still have something to long after, and the weak may not draw back in alarm" (Ch 64). This, indeed, is discretion, "the mother of the virtues".

The recognition of one's inadequacy is the first step towards acquiring humility, which is the basis of Benedictine spirituality. Humility is facing the truth. The monk knows deep-down that he is not what he should be, not just in terms of his monastic vocation, but as a human being like everyone else. It takes some years of experience in monastic life to recognise that consciousness of failure and frailty must not lead to despondency, but rather to complete trust and confidence in God's help. We have to move from preoccupation with our own perfection to an intense interest in the perfection of God. There is a double process that goes on all the time: increasingly we identify with that poor tax collector, whose prayer was "Lord, be merciful to me a sinner", whilst, at the same time, there grows the conviction that God's love for us is strong, warm and intimate. It is this which calls forth from us a response of love – *abyssus invocat abyssum*. The abyss of our nothingness has to be filled with the immensity of God's love. Humility is a lovable virtue – delightful to observe in others; painfully difficult to acquire for oneself. But it is the only way to get the relationships in the monastery right: that is, between God and ourselves on the one hand, and between the brethren on the other. Proud men cannot live together in peace.

As the monk struggles painfully to become truly humble, he will come, so the Rule teaches, to that perfect love of God which casts out all fear (Ch 7). How very important it is to recognise that humility, as St Benedict understands it, is a whole attitude of mind. The false idea that the humble man is, in some way, an emaciated person, limp and negative, would have been far from his thought. On the contrary, humility is a virtue for the strong monk, because it enables him to put God and other people at the centre of his life, and not himself. It should release the powers and energies with which God has endowed him, and make him a valuable instrument in the service of the Lord. Monks have to be good human beings; the proud are not.

The Rule warns monks against two tendencies which can ruin the individual's spiritual life and are corrosive of community living. The first tendency is the problem of self-will. "We are, indeed, forbidden to do our own will by Scripture, which says to us: 'Turn away from thine own will.' Moreover we ask God in prayer that His will be done in us" (Ch 7) – so the Rule says. This passage sums up one of the guiding principles for the monk: it is God's will that he must seek and not his own. The kind of docility which St Benedict's strictures about self-will seem to propose is not always easy for a lively and intelligent twentieth-century monk to accept. But there is a false docility, which reduces a man, and a correct one, which is

a new strength. St Benedict is speaking of a docility which
is a surrendering to God's will, or, better, a manly embrac-
ing of it.

One problem in monastic life is the conflict between, on
the one hand, the lawful drive in a normal person which
should lead to creative achievement, and on the other, the
duties imposed by obedience and the needs of the community. It is the tension between what is demanded of the
monk by others and the pursuit by him of private and personal aims, ambitions and inspirations. The danger is ever
present of the monk making himself the centre of his
monastic life, and not God. This is, as we well know, the
original sin. Obedience certainly saves the monk from self-
seeking and self-centredness; attitudes which are destructive of true love. The gift the monk makes of himself at
the time of his profession, has to be total and radical and
never withdrawn. The finest monks I have known did
precisely this; many of the unhappy ones did not. A wise
Abbot, I presume, will always guide a monk in the direction in which the monk's talents and inclination would
normally lead him. It is a strange kind of spirituality, and
a perverse one, that would wish to impose an obedience
which does violence to a man's temperament and gifts.
Nevertheless, the monk for his part must be prepared to
do what is uncongenial, and work for which he would regard himself as temperamentally unsuited, if it is asked of
him – and certainly be prepared for it. There can be no
conditions laid down, or contemplated, at the time of profession.

The second tendency which is harmful in the monastic
life, is the fault known as "murmuring". That word betrays
a whole attitude of mind which is in direct contradiction
to the monastic way. It would be inconceivable to have a
monastery in which there were not several very justifiable
reasons for grumbling and discontent. No need for me to
labour the point.

A new problem has arisen today as a result of the call for "renewal" in the Church and in religious life. It has not been easy for monastic communities to find a common mind as to what "renewal" means and what should be done to achieve it. Self-examination and self-criticism have been necessary, no doubt, but a community can become too preoccupied with the process, and the potential danger of divisions and dissatisfaction are all too obvious. The dialogue of the Chapter-house can so easily degenerate into grumbling in the cloister. Dialogue, at its best, is positive and constructive; grumbling, of its nature, is negative and destructive. "Discretion", that characteristic word of the Rule, applies in this situation, as in so many others, and this "discretion" is, I believe, the "prudence" of which St Thomas speaks: the right means to achieve the desired end.

So we may now leave our consideration of the "earthenware vessels" and move on to speak of the monastic ideal. What follows now is, doubtless, only a personal view, but then I have no other to offer.

The account of the early Christian community given in the Acts of the Apostles would provide – and in many cases has provided – an obvious starting-point from which to look at the monastic ideal. However, I have preferred to begin by considering the nature of man, and especially the final end of that nature, and to allow my thoughts on the monastic ideal to flow from that. It is only one of several possible options and, I trust, a legitimate one. No monastery will work if its way of life is founded upon an erroneous anthropology. It will not be on the right lines unless it is consistent with what man is, and with what man is for. Furthermore, the monastic life, since it is one way of living out the original baptismal commitment, must too, express the fundamental values and precepts of the Gospel.

I take as my starting-point man as a being who is in

need of fulfilment, and as such, is in search of those things
which will satisfy him.

Man has many needs. He is a creature of desires. Two
in particular characterise him insofar as he is human: let
us call them the search for meaning and the desire for
happiness. Both these basic drives are strong and deep. In
the search for meaning, the mind is seeking its object,
which is truth; in the search for happiness, the will desires
its object, which is the good. The satisfaction of the mind's
restless enquiry consists in knowledge and understanding;
the greatest moments of human happiness are the experi-
ences of love, when wanting gives way to the possession of
the good desired. To know and to love, these are pre-eminently and specifically human activities. Add to these, the
recognition of, and delight in, the true and the good, then
beauty has been discovered. Truth and goodness in their
absolute forms are found in God alone; the awareness of
them, in so far as this is possible to us in our present state,
is to have seen something of His glory, which is beauty at
its purest, with neither blemish nor distortion. The beauty
of God, seen directly, will elicit from us that gasp of wonder and admiration, which will be our eternal praising of
His glory. The knowledge of God as He is in Himself, the
love that will flow from that vision, and the song of wonder must inevitably follow – these define the final purpose
of man.

We are not there yet. We remain pilgrims through life,
limping along the road, but buoyant, nevertheless in the
knowledge of what shall one day be ours. At present we
are pilgrims in search of God. We come to the monastery
to seek Him.

The final purpose of man, and thus clearly of the monk
as well, determines his priorities while still a pilgrim in
this world; namely, to know God, and knowing Him, to
love Him and praise Him. This explains the task of the
monk. His function is to seek God, and in no way to flinch

from the difficulties which the search will entail. You will recall what St Benedict requires of the novice: he is to be examined as to "whether he truly seeks God, and whether he is zealous for the work of God, for obedience, and for humiliations (*opprobria*)" (Ch 58). And we may understand, too, why such prominence is given in the Rule to *lectio divina*, to the *opus Dei* and to the monastery as the *schola servitii Domini*. These three correspond to the purpose of man which is to know God, to praise Him and to serve Him.

The motive for service must be love. The greatest happiness is the experience of love. It is to know that which is most lovable, and to possess and be possessed by that. The most lovable of all that is lovable is God. It is not surprising, then, that at the heart of the Christian life is the command to love the Lord our God. That command is not simply a precept that comes to us from the outside; it expresses the very law of our human nature. It tells us how to be fully human. How right it is, then, that the first "tool of good works" in the Rule states quite simply: "in the first place, to love the Lord God with all one's heart, all one's soul and all one's strength" (Ch 4). That gives meaning to all the other "tools of good works".

I do not think that we can stress enough the part that the love of God must have in our monastic lives. It seems very obvious to state it simply like this; after all we know it to be fundamental to our Christian response to the love which has first been shown to us. How far do we give only notional and not real assent to the proposition that union with God is, ultimately, the true purpose of man? To know God, and to be known by Him; to want Him, and to recognise that He wants us; to realise that He alone can satisfy our desire to be with and for another ... do we really assent to this? Marriage and friendship lead people much of the way towards discovering the meaning of love in God, but they cannot take us the whole way. They are foretastes of

future bliss, but not yet the real thing. Indeed, this last
observation does less than justice to the dignity of human
love, for not only is it a way of discovering the meaning of
the word "love" as it is used of God, but in some manner,
it is part of it. But love's final triumph comes later on; it is
the moment when God possesses us fully.

There is no need here to work out the link between the
first and second commandments, as they are given to us by
the Lord, and so admirably explained by St John in his
first letter. St Benedict puts the love of our neighbour
second among the "tools". The reason for stressing the
second commandment is because it must be the basis of
our community life. It is the art of relating to one another
as brothers. It provides, too, the reason – apart from the
laudable one of earning our living – for the good works
which the monastery may undertake. It is Christ whom we
must see and serve, not only in the Abbot, the poor and the
sick, but in each of those with whom we come into contact.
In the baptised, we find Christ, for it is by His life that they
now live, and in the non-baptised, for in them Christ wishes
to be. This is the doctrine of St Paul, following the teaching of the Lord Himself, which finds its way into the Rule,
and, in more recent times, was a constant theme in the
writings of Abbot Columba Marmion.

These reflections prompt two thoughts about community
life; first, it is salutary to remember that it is one thing to
live with a group of men of like mind and outlook, and
with whom we have a natural affinity; it is quite another
to live and work with men whom we would not normally
choose as obvious companions. I recall my predecessor as
Abbot telling us once, with his customary directness and
alarming perspicacity: "Do remember, Fathers, that when
you die, someone will be relieved." That may shock,
but it makes a telling point. We are reminded that although
we are social animals, we are also wounded creatures.

Tolerance and patience are indispensable qualities for every monk. "Let monks, therefore, exercise this zeal with the most fervent love. Let them, that is, in honour prefer one another. Let them bear with the greatest patience one another's infirmities, whether of body or character. Let them vie in paying obedience one to another ..." (Ch 72). Only secure people, with a high degree of human and spiritual maturity, are able to maintain that kind of standard day in and day out. I speak as one of the "earthenware vessels".

St Benedict, in that same chapter 72, says: "Let them practise fraternal charity with all purity." There is no need to speak at length about that to this particular audience; except to remind ourselves that a celibate's relationships both inside and outside the monastery must be warm and human, but controlled and restrained. Indeed, the love of which I have been speaking, is the generous and giving kind, rich and rewarding because it is not grasping or selfish. For us it is the joy of friendship. That is an art to be learned.

We cannot conclude these thoughts on the "monastic ideal" without considering the work of the monastery, and the involvement of many monasteries in work which is very demanding in terms of time and energy. There is a passage in St Augustine where he writes: *otium sanctum quaerit caritas veritatis: negotium justum suscipit necessitas caritatis* (De Civ. Dei XIX, 19) – "the love of truth seeks a holy leisure, but the urgency of love undertakes the work that is due." That sums up neatly the tension that there can be between a life dedicated wholly to prayer, and a life which is involved in considerable activity. St Augustine is referring to persons who are ordained to the episcopate, but his words can apply equally well to those in the monastic life. St Augustine goes on to say, and this is important, that even if the burden of the episcopacy is undertaken because of the "urgency of love", nonetheless, all delight "in the truth" must not be abandoned. The sweetness of that delight must remain.

Some are called to the desert, not so much to flee from the world with its possible threats and dangers, but rather because they are drawn to that direct search for God, which, traditionally, we term the contemplative life, that is, a life in which prayer and silence play the greatest and predominant part. It is good that the Rule has given rise to such a life, both within our own Confederation and outside it. But what of the rest of us, with our schools and other pastoral work? Historically, monasticism has always received guests, welcomed the poor, and shared its riches with others. The problem has always been to keep the right balance between prayer, *lectio divina* and work. Reform, or renewal, consists in readjusting this delicate equilibrium.

Allow me to make two further points: first, there are many monks who are simply not capable of leading a life consisting of long periods of prayer and manual work. They need to be stimulated by more challenging work, or by a greater pastoral involvement. The flexibility of our tradition has made it possible for these men, too, to search for God in their way. I say "their way", but this is not completely accurate; it is a question of vocation, the way that God seems to call them. Secondly, the work done in school or otherwise must flow from a life of prayer. That is central and fundamental, no need to elaborate on this point.

The monastic life that is dedicated to prayer almost exclusively is to be respected and treasured, but that life which involves the monk in hard and selfless work for others has its value, too. It is not less virtuous than the former; it is different.

I doubt whether there are many of us, if any, who can look back on our monastic lives without some tinge of regret. That should not be surprising. The "treasure" which we were given, our monastic vocation, is contained in "perishable earthenware". St Paul makes the point that matters: "It must be God and not anything in ourselves, that gives it its sovereign power" (2 Cor. 4:7). If the regrets show us our limitations, what we have lost through negligence we shall retrieve through our sorrow. One day we shall see Him as He is – the hours spent in the choir will have prepared us for the eternity we shall spend in our praising of Him, and our works of love, done for Him and for His sons and daughters, will have fashioned us for that moment of ecstatic love, which is for the monk, as for all who seek God, His eternal reward.

We do not set out upon the journey of discovery, as pilgrims, alone. It is with and through Jesus Christ, our way, our truth, and our life that we walk, for the monastic way leads us, or should do, to be His disciples. The Holy Spirit has been sent to us to involve us in the mystery of God who became man, so that we may attain, one day, to that vision of God, when He will be our all.

Ealing Abbey, London
21 March, 1980

It would be difficult, I believe, to walk far in our country without treading on ground that has not been, at some period in history, known to, or even cultivated by, monks. Great tracts of land were cleared and drained by monks, and especially by Cistercians, our country's first great sheep farmers. Go into our cities and towns and see the great cathedrals and churches – Canterbury, Worcester, Durham, and many others – and be reminded, once again, of our monastic past. Ancient libraries treasure manuscripts which were painstakingly hand-copied by monks, and great works which were written in those medieval monasteries. More important are the great men and women whose names we honour in our Benedictine calendar. There are too many to mention individually here, but they provide us with a lengthy litany of saints, intercessors on our behalf to this very day, and examples to us, their successors, of what we ourselves should be.

None of these achievements could possibly have been foreseen by St Benedict when he left his home in Nurcia to pursue his studies in Rome. Indeed, the world of learning and the town life of the fifth century proved not to be for him. He was disgusted by what he saw around him in Rome, and, as his biographer St Gregory wrote: "He left the world, being knowingly unknowing and wisely unlearned." It was the life of a hermit that St Benedict then sought, a life of silence and solitude, away from people and from the business of everyday living. He retreated to a cave high up on a hillside by a lake, alone, save for the visit of a monk called Romanus, who provided him with food and, no doubt, with spiritual guidance as well. Once established in his cave, St Benedict must have thought that this at last was to be his vocation. Never for a moment could he have thought of himself as a great reformer, or considered himself as the kind of person who could put the world to rights. He would have smiled, I think, if you had told him that one day he was to be regarded as the Father of all the monks in the West; that one day a Pope, Paul VI, would proclaim him a patron of Europe. Indeed, he would have laughed aloud in disbelief! And yet this was how it was to be. It is not our plans and ideas, but God's plan that matters. We may think and plan one way; God generally arranges things quite otherwise.

Benedict was not left alone and solitary for long. His reputation grew – being spread by the local shepherds – and others wanted to live lives consecrated to God. Disciples sought him out. Eventually, by that lake in Subiaco, Benedict was compelled to found his first monastery – twelve groups of men who devoted their lives to prayer. It was a kind of monastic village. There he remained until the year 529 when, after trouble with a local priest, he left and went to live – and to found the monastery – on Monte Cassino. Here he ruled, and gave his monks a Rule of life. In fact, there had been monks in the Church for two hundred years before St Benedict's time, and there were many Rules by which monks could live. Our patron chose one of these and made some changes in it and so produced what we today know as the "Rule of St Benedict".

Again, St Benedict had no idea that others would take over his Rule, but by the year A.D. 800 there was in fact no other rule for monks. This was largely due to the Emperor Charlemagne, a man who liked good order, and apparently, a good deal of uniformity as well. There will in future, so he decreed, be only one rule and that will be St Benedict's. Those who advised the Emperor knew what they were doing, for the Rule of St Benedict was popular and many monasteries used it. In England it had probably already been known at the time of St Augustine's arrival in 597, but it was St Wilfrid who was largely responsible for its becoming the standard Rule for monasteries from the second half of the seventh century onwards.

So, St Benedict did not mean to found an Order. In this he is unlike many later saints – such as St Francis or St Ignatius; nor did he intend to write the Rule for any save his own monks at Monte Cassino. These facts, to me at any rate, say something important about the Benedictines. We do not see ourselves as having any particular mission or function in the Church. We do not set out to change the course of history. We are just there – almost by accident from a human point of view. And, happily, we go on "just being there". Our past now stretches back nearly fifteen centuries, and, under God, we have in that time made our contribution to the work of Christ, and in doing this we have left our mark.... This centenary of St Benedict's birth provides us, the monks, and you, our friends, with an opportunity to thank God for giving Benedict to the world and for what God in His goodness, has enabled Benedict's followers to do.

Since St Benedict did not intend his Rule to have application beyond his own monastery, why has the Rule been such a success? Why has so much been achieved through it and because of it? Oddly enough, St Benedict seems not to have had much opinion of his monks. In his view, the monks of his days were a sorry lot compared with those who preceded them. In the old days monks were tougher and better ... Monks, for example, should not drink wine at all, but if nowadays they must, then, said St Benedict, please do it in moderation. The lives of monks used to be a perpetual Lent, but in these days, he says, if it is no longer so, at least make a special effort when that season does come round. Formerly, monks recited all 150 psalms

each day; well, nowadays, let them at least recite them
each week ...

In all this, I think, we have another of the Benedictine
secrets: monks are ordinary people, on the whole. We are
not spiritually star performers. So the Rule of St Benedict
makes it possible for ordinary folk to live lives of quite
extraordinary value. The weak have a place to do their
best ...

This importance of the weak and the ordinary is one of
the great guiding principles of the Rule and determines
how the Abbot is to handle people. The Rule says: "So,
taking these and other examples of discretion, the mother
of the virtues, let him so temper all things that the strong
may still have something to long after, and the weak may
not draw back in alarm." How important it is not to treat
people equally nor to attempt to mould them into one set
pattern. The Rule demands that monks be seen as individuals, each precious in the sight of God, and the Rule is
full of compassion.

In this sixth-century document, there is then much
understanding of the way human beings function. For example, St Benedict's two chapters on the Abbot provide
principles and guidance which could be adopted by any-
body who holds a position of authority in any walk of life.
What he says about community life, too, is full of wisdom
and shrewd commonsense. Even today, then, St Benedict
has something helpful to say to us as we strive in our
modern world to find new modes of leadership and new
ways of living in community.

Wise, moderate, compassionate: these are the characteristics of the Rule of St Benedict, and they are surely
qualities which St Benedict himself had in abundance. St
Gregory tells us that Benedict lived himself what he had
written. In any age these three qualities should be
honoured, and not least in our own. And I believe that the
success of St Benedict's Rule is partly due to the presence

of these characteristics and their exercise in favour of the
weak and the ordinary.

When we come to consider why the Rule has made
possible so many achievements, it is harder to make objec-
tive judgments. One thought attracts me. If you ask anyone who is knowledgeable about Church matters, to name
two or three Benedictines who are world-famous, he would
not be able to get further than mentioning a name or two
from some Benedictine community known to him. On the
whole, monks do not become famous – and that is a good
thing – but monasteries do – and that is an excellent
thing. In other words, it is the community that matters. It
is as a member of a community that the individual monk
does his particular job. It is within the monastic family
that he grows and learns, develops his talents and is supported ... And all this is achieved under the guidance of
the Abbot whose role in the monastery is crucial. He must
truly be what the word "abbot" means – a "father".

We have still to answer the question: what is the secret
of the success of a monastery? There are two interrelated
causes. First, there is the central part which prayer does,
and must, play in the life of the monastery and in the life
of each monk. The praise of God, day in, day out, all the
year round, this is always the main work of the community, the *opus Dei*. If this ceases to be so, then the
effectiveness of the monastery diminishes. Secondly, the
dedication to living the Gospel is equally important. The
monk comes to the monastery to seek God, and this he
does, like any other Christian, by becoming a follower of
Christ. The monastic life is one way of being a Christian,
not chosen by us but followed because we have discovered
that God has called us to this rather than to any other
Christian way of life. As monks we bind ourselves to follow Christ by our vows: of obedience, of stability within a
particular monastery, and to try to achieve that degree of
holiness which God wishes for us. Love of our vows, by

giving us inner freedom and dedication to do God's will, enables us to serve Christ in our neighbour. Put succinctly, we may say that the sole purpose of a monk is to love God above all things and his neighbour as himself. That, after all, is simply the heart of the Christian life – a Gospel command – and so these two loves, which indeed are only one, must be in the heart of every monk.

The "love of our neighbour" – that outpouring of the love of God, or at least our striving to know what this means – leads us to see Christ in the guest who knocks at our doors, and in the poor, especially, who are in need of our help. The riches of the monastery, whether spiritual or material, are to be shared with others. A monastery may well appear to be a barrier – indeed, in a sense, it is symbolically so, for the values by which many people in the world live must not be the values of the monk – but the door must be open, and the porter welcoming.

It is this idea of "sharing the riches of the monastery" and of welcoming the stranger, which explains the traditional role of our monasteries in, say, the field of education. Our schools are, in a way, an extension of our hospitality. In any case, we must earn our living. Our Benedictine schools do have special characteristics: the pursuit of excellence; the family spirit; the priority of the spiritual; "humanist" in the proper sense, we aim to educate boys, and sometimes, happily, girls, into being good human beings with strong faith and ease of manner in the presence of God and in the adult world. We do not always succeed, of course, but there is no doubt about the value of the work.

And the local community in which our monasteries are situated must, too, be served. At Ealing, set as it is in an urban situation, the need is all the more clear, and necessary. We are proud of this Benedictine parish in this diocese, one of two, for I do not forget our brethren at Cockfosters, nor those who work in Hendon.

There is always, then, around any monastic community, that larger community composed of parishioners and members of the school, relations and friends, visitors from near and far. They all constitute that larger Benedictine family which supports and is supported by the monks of the monastery. This makes our celebration this year, 1980, so special for so many people, and it is good that in this abbey church of St Benedict's Ealing, we, the friends of the community should come together to join them in their praising of God, and to pray that the monks here may be richly blessed and rewarded for all that they do for all of us.

St Louis Cathedral, St Louis, USA
1 June, 1980

My first word must be one of gratitude to you, Archbishop May, as the bishop of this great See, and in the very same breath, to His Eminence the Cardinal, now a friend of several years, and a dear one, too. It is gracious of you, Archbishop, to allow me to be the principal celebrant in your cathedral on this occasion. I greet you, your priests and people on behalf of the priests and people of the diocese of Westminster. We shall pray that your pastoral ministry here in St Louis will be richly blessed by Almighty God.

How right it is that we should be praying together and meeting together, for collegiality is strengthened, not only when we come together in formal sessions, but especially so when we welcome each other into our respective dioceses and share our common concern for all the churches.

Your presence, and the presence of other bishops too, reminds us, the religious men and women, that our lives, dedicated to God through our vows, are to be lived in the Church and for the Church. Our role, as religious, is to be part of the Church's prophetic voice, a reminder, under God, of the values of that Kingdom of God which strives to be in the city of man. The sons and daughters of St Benedict have special reasons for gratitude to the bishop of this diocese, for it was by the kind permission and with the encouragement of their Eminences, Cardinals Ritter and Carberry that three of the communities here today were able to settle and work in this diocese.

So here we are, bishops, priests, religious and people assembled together to praise and thank God for the life of

St Benedict, and for the influence he has had through count-
less men and women, who have followed *his* Rule in *their*
way of becoming disciples of Christ, their way of living
the Gospel. The monastic life is, indeed, one way, and
one only, of being a Christian, not chosen by us, but followed because we have discovered that God has called us
to this rather than to any other way. We bind ourselves
to follow Christ by our vows: of stability within a particular monastic family, of obedience to seek and to do only
what is God's will, and we pledge ourselves to that constant change of heart, away from false values and aspirations to the discovery of the mystery which God is. Put
succinctly, we may say that the sole purpose of the monk
is to love God above all things and his neighbour as himself. That, after all, is simply the heart of the Christian life
– it is the Gospel command.

As you well know, St Benedict had no intention of
founding a religious order; that way of thinking belongs to
a much later age. Indeed he himself started life as a hermit,
and it was at the request of others that he accepted disciples, first at Subiaco and later at Monte Cassino. How
should these disciples live? St Benedict studied ancient
Rules and consulted previous monastic experiments, and he
adapted the former practices to the needs of his monks, and
this became known as the Rule of St Benedict. A wise,
moderate and compassionate document, it mirrored, as St
Gregory the Great tells us, the very characteristics of Benedict himself. It became the standard Rule for all monks
and nuns, gradually gaining favour simply because it
worked, then by imperial decree the Emperor Charlemagne
declared that it alone should be used. But St Benedict was
only thinking of his monks at Monte Cassino. And what
did he expect them to do?

I suppose it is true to say that St Benedict did not see the
Benedictines as having any particular mission or function
within the Church. In fact, we have never set out to

change the course of history. We were just there, almost by accident, seen from a human point of view. We go on "just being there". Our past stretches back nearly fifteen hundred years, and happily under God, we have in that time made our contribution to the work of Christ.

The monk was to seek God – the organisation of the monastery and the spiritual doctrines contained in the Rule were ordered to that, to that first and to that above all. And this is so important. The monk sets out from the day of his admission to the monastery on a journey of exploration. It is to explore the mystery which God is; it is an attempt to catch a glimpse of His glory, insofar as this is possible in our present state; it is a longing to discover something of the strong and warm love which the Father has for His sons and daughters; it is a listening to the word which He speaks through the Scriptures, and to that word which can be heard in the depths of our being. Rare, perhaps are the moments when a ray of light breaks through the cloud of unknowing to enlighten the mind and to warm that heart, but often sufficient to reward fidelity and to give courage in moments of darkness. Enough, too, to inspire our song of praise, for this – preeminently for us the work of God – is central to our monastic ideal. We do it several times a day; nothing is to be preferred to it. Man is made to praise God, and he is truly himself when so engaged – even when the weakness of our natures makes the song less than totally spontaneous. Darkness is a joy when it heralds the arrival of the light. My dear monastic brethren and sisters, never doubt the value of that work of praise – and, if I may add a personal plea to this rather pretentious appeal by me to you – remind us who do not live in the monastery of the importance of reverence and dignity when we place ourselves in the presence of God to do His work. To perceive beauty in the worshipping of God is to enable us to catch sight, for a moment, of that beauty of God, which is His glory.

The monastic community becomes over the years a great reservoir of spiritual riches, and from it the waters of life must flow to water the arid wastes of a world that is thirsting for God. It has always been so, and must be thus today. A monastic community is the meeting point of much giving, of the brethren or sisters to each other, and of each one and all collectively to God Himself. The reservoir is fed by individual streams. The outpourings of those rivers of life are the flowing forth of love. Those riches are to be shared – by those who come to pray with us. With the strangers who knock at our doors and especially with the poor, with those who come to be educated by us or with those whom we go out to serve. Many of our friends are praying with us here today, and it is right to acknowledge support given and love received. A monastic community extends beyond its professed membership. You, too, our friends, are streams that help to fill the reservoir of spiritual riches. We thank you for that.

May these schools of the Lord's service prosper and be blessed by God – St Pius X, the Sisters of Perpetual Adoration, Our Lady of Peace Convent of Columba Missouri, and the Priory of St Louis – I think, too, of the communities of Acheson, of Conception, of St Procopius and of St Meinrad's, and many, many others in the United States.

I have said enough, and we must now proceed to offer up this great Sacrifice, which is the Mass and share together the one bread and the one cup – on a great Feast day, the feast of the Blessed Trinity. As I conclude I hear the voice of that person of the Trinity, calling to us from the Cross, and as He does so, He expresses the appealing cry of God to return the love which He has first given to us. The voice cries: "I thirst" – it thirsts for you and for me, and that divine thirst cannot be satisfied until He has found and discovered us.

Archabbey of St Vincent's, Latrobe, USA
11 June, 1980

I wonder what it was that St Benedict saw as he looked out at night from his room in the tower. Serandus, the deacon, lay asleep in the room below. They had finished their conversation when they had been speaking of sacred things, so that they might "at least taste in words of yearning desire the delights of heaven which they could not yet perfectly enjoy". St Benedict had seen a great light, "and the whole world had seemed as if gathered into one sunbeam, and brought thus before his eyes". *"Animae videnti creatorem"* wrote St Gregory, *"angusta est omnis creatura"* – to a soul that sees the Creator all creation becomes small. St Benedict's biographer then goes on: "Though it see but a glimpse of the light of the Creator all that is created becomes little in its eyes. By the light of that inward vision the grasp of the mind is so extended and enlarged in God that it transcends the word" (Ch 35). And we might add, by way of our own commentary on this strange event, once we have achieved but a glimpse of the glory of God, we can see the world, its people and events, in their true perspective, that is, as they truly are.

The character and personality of St Benedict, as we piece it together from interpreting the Rule, and from picking our way through the *Dialogues* of St Gregory, slowly emerges, even if neither source be, in fact, historical in a strictly scientific sense. Fear and respect in the presence of God, the primacy of the demands which God makes upon us, a deep love of Christ, and so sincerity, compassion and good sense are some the qualities that characterise the Saint. I see him as a man for whom God is all, serene,

calm and totally free. If we did not know something of the
world in which he lived we might be tempted to think
that St Benedict lived unaffected by the events of his day.
Such a view would be quite erroneous.

St Benedict lived in a turbulent period of history. Only
four years before his birth the line of the Western Emperors officially came to an end. Caesar lived in Byzantium,
no longer in Rome; and until Justinian's rule was finally
established in 555 Rome was ruled by barbarian kings –
"My voice is choked and sobs interrupt the words which
I write; the city is captured which took captive the world
– *capitur urbs quae totum cepit orbem*," lamented St
Jerome from his cave in Bethlehem. Alaric had sacked
Rome in 410, Genseric in 455. What we call Italy today,
from then onwards, knew the alternating rhythm of war
and peace. Not that all was loss and anguish, for the dying
days of the Roman Empire knew from time to time peaceful interludes. Internal decay and external attack had taken
their toll. Much was going wrong, and there was drought
and famine, notably in 538, which caused St Benedict to
rebuke, and rebuke severely, a cellarer who – as I would
think – was only trying to do his best for the monks. He
had refused to give up the only oil they had. Unfortunately
he acted in contradiction to his vow of obedience. That
never works, as we all eventually discover.

Many of the troubles that surrounded him in the society
of his day are reflected in the saint's own personal life.
Things did not always work out as he had anticipated.
After all, he had set out for Rome from his family home
in Nurcia to study in the great city; but it was too corrupt,
and he moved on to get away from it all. Then the call to
the eremitical life was strong, and so he scrambled to the
cave at Subiaco and accepted the kind ministrations of
the monk Romanus. It was not to last – he was forced
to get involved in the coenobitical life. One thing is certain; whatever the state of that first monastery at Vicovaro,

Benedict did not succeed in winning over the community to which he first went. They did not take to their new Abbot, and planned a most drastic means of ridding themselves of him. Poisoned wine would achieve their wicked aim; but it did not work; St Benedict blessed the cup, and it broke. Vicovaro is, in many ways, a consoling episode for us Abbots, when things go wrong. I doubt whether any of our communities would sink to the mediocrity of that community, but it is consoling to know that even Benedict could not get those monks to renew. Nor was he always liked by his neighbours. A turbulent and jealous priest succeeded in driving Benedict away from Subiaco. He also tried to poison him, this time with bread. Thanks to that episode, the foundation at Monte Cassino was made possible. The broken wine cup and the poisoned bread – so I reflect – were countersigns, as it were, of that unity which should have prevailed in those two monastic communities, and which is so significantly shown forth when the monks share the one cup and the one bread of the Holy Eucharist. Things did not always run smoothly at Monte Cassino, but all the time, so we may assume, he who lived as he taught, must have been quietly scaling those twelve steps to humility, and learning, in the school of the Lord's service, the love of God and of his neighbour, which lie right in the heart of the Gospel and so he began "to run with unspeakable sweetness of love in the way of God's commandments" (Prologue H.B.). All the stories about St Benedict, granted the special purpose of his biographer, reveal him to have been a man who won the admiration and confidence of all who heard of him or knew him. He was indeed full of the spirit of all the just; he was a man of God.

What of us fifteen hundred years later? No Abbot, no monk, no Benedictine nun or sister sees life work out quite as it might have been envisaged during the novitiate days. Obedience can lead us into strange and, sometimes not totally congenial occupations. We have our temperaments with which to contend, and events in the monastery and in the world around us, which can disorientate and worry us. There are other periods, happily many of them, when things go smoothly and, we are naturally at peace and at ease. We thank God for both situations, for all the time we are learning to keep our minds and our hearts on God, on His mercy and His love. We, too, may be given from time to time some share of the vision, so that, slowly we realise that "to the souls that see the Creator all creation becomes small". We follow St Benedict, not only in the spiritual doctrine that he gives us, but along the way which he himself has to tread, and especially in our love of the vows, and on the ladder that leads to true humility. We accept the *dura* and the *aspera*. They are part of every human life.

As we look round the world in which our monasteries are situated, we do not allow ourselves to be depressed, nor do we condemn or criticise from an Olympian height. Compared with God His creation is small, but that does not mean that it is unimportant or of no significance. Indeed, seen as God sees it, we value it, for God Himself does so. As the Roman Empire became medieval Europe, the sons of St Benedict preserved learning and civilised their environment, and so contributed to passing to the future the best of the past. That is our task today. The contribution that we can make is very important. Allow me to develop one aspect of it.

I think that we are beginning to discover that the great technological and scientific achievements of our age, cannot eliminate or resolve the great questions, which men and women have always asked themselves right down the ages, I mean about the meaning and purpose of life, about suffering, about death, and we are slowly realising that the values of what has been called the "consumer society" cannot satisfy our deepest and noblest aspirations. In short, we are learning, once again, that a world without God does not work. Our monasteries are affirmations of God, of the Gospel, of spiritual values. These must be clear to all. The stranger who comes to the monastery, those with whom we share our riches, in our colleges and schools, should see us striving to be men of God, because we are men of faith and prayer. We must not go to sleep, like Serandus, but be ever watchful looking for the light, with yearning desire for the delights of heaven which we cannot perfectly enjoy yet. Then we shall have something to give men and women of our day, who although not acknowledging it, nevertheless are unconsciously in search for that which gives meaning to all things and for that happiness and peace which a restless world cannot give.

We, monks and sisters, have an important, indeed a vital role to play in the life of the Church. We must speak to men and women of our society about God and the things of God, and this we shall do by living the Gospel and communicating it by our example, by our attitudes, by our teaching. This is what is meant, surely, by presence and witness. St Benedict has given us one way of doing this. We must be ourselves, combining the virtues of humility and modesty with confidence in ourselves. You have many riches in your Congregation; this has been quite evident to us who have been privileged to have been your guests these last few days. Treasure those riches, and share them when you are asked to do so.

Of course there are problems, and grave ones, in the world today. It was so in St Benedict's time. Of course in your monastic lives, either as communities or as individuals, things do not always work out as you had expected or hoped. St Benedict knew that kind of thing as well. We are in God's hands, and those hands are good and strong.

I hear St Benedict saying to us what he said to the astonished Goth, who had just retrieved the instrument he had lost. "There now, work on, and be sad no longer –

"ecce labora et noli contristari" (Dialogues Ch 6). That is no bad motto for our centenary year: *"ecce labora et noli contristari"*. Work on and be full of joy, for God is well pleased with our efforts. Keep watching from the tower, look outwards and around you, and you, too, will see a light, not the full light, perhaps, which St Benedict saw, but the glow that followed it, and was glimpsed by the deacon, Serandus, once he had been roused from his sleep – a small light, but enough.

The National Shrine of the Immaculate Conception, Washington, USA
15 June, 1980

Has St Benedict a message for the modern world?

That is a question which has been put to me on many occasions since we began to celebrate the fifteenth centenary of his birth. I suspect that there are many possible different answers to that question. I suspect, too, incidentally that St Benedict would have thought it a foolish question, but that reflection is unimportant.

Fifteen hundred years is a long time, and things are very different now. Look at what we have achieved since the time of St Benedict; see what has been discovered by scientific research and accomplished by technological expertise. We have probed into the secrets of the universe and discovered, latent there, powers and possibilities undreamed of by our forefathers. We are right to acknowledge work done by those who have gone before us, right to be proud of their and our success, right to praise God for the genius which is man.

The inventions of man, whether they be of ancient times or of our own, can speak to us of the power and glory of God. We were commanded to use our God-given gifts and talents. "Yahweh God took man and settled him in the garden of Eden to cultivate and take care of it", so we read in an early chapter of the book of Genesis (Gen 2:15). The world was meant to be a garden of Eden, we were supposed to work at it and to "take care of it". Have we really done so? What in fact have we to show for all our skill and knowledge?

There is in our society today a great dilemma: great skill and power in our hands on the one hand, our in-

ability to get things right on the other. We seem to be
curiously inept when it comes to arranging things on this
planet.

We were commanded to cultivate the garden and take
care of it, so that all men, women and children should be
enabled to live in peace, each with what was necessary for
life, the human dignity of every person respected and
protected, peace prevailing because the tranquillity of
order was wanted and treasured by all. Such was the vision
at the beginning of time. Man's foolishness has made it
otherwise. Is it right, indeed is it not folly, that there
should be such disparity of wealth between the rich and
poor countries? Should all those millions of people go
hungry, many starving to death? Why do we exploit and
pollute the atmosphere, the soil and the sea, and use up
so voraciously our reserves of energy, and so risk crisis
upon crisis? And what of that terrible power that can
destroy whole peoples, perhaps even exterminate the whole
human race? And why do we fail to reverence and protect
human life, and kill the unborn and give ourselves over
to conflict, to violence, to war?

The greatest folly of all – and it is the cause of the others
just mentioned – is to forget that above us and beyond us,
there is a voice that calls us all the time to a change of
heart, and to a new beginning. Happily that voice does not
always go unheeded, for I believe that there are many who
hear and listen to that voice deep down within themselves.
They have experienced the need to hear a word which will
give meaning, and purpose to human existence. That is
not surprising, for we are, after all, by nature religious
creatures, though we often do not recognise it, seldom,
perhaps, acknowledge it, sometimes, even, fight against it.
There is in each one of us a divine spark, never totally
extinguished, but always in need of rekindling. Man is
made for God.

Now it does not help, nor is it sensible, just to criticise

our society, lament its abuses and curse its ills. We live
in an age of great complexity – issues, whether political,
social or economic, are never entirely black or entirely
white; people, by and large, are never wholly good, never
wholly bad. But if the best is to be brought out of them,
they need hope, and there is no hope where there is no
vision. You may recall how the Brandt Report states:
"New generations need not simply economic solutions,
but ideas to inspire them, hopes to encourage them, initial
steps to implement those ideas and hopes." Man does not
live by bread alone. But if, in the words of the prophet
Joel, "our sons and daughters are to prophesy, our old
men dream dreams, and our young see visions" (Joel
2:28), then we must needs stir ourselves.

"Now is the hour for us to rise from sleep", so we read
in the Prologue to the Rule of St Benedict, "let us open
our eyes to the divine light, and let us hear with attentive
ears the warning that the divine voice crieth daily to us:
'Today if you will hear his voice, harden not your hearts'"
(Ps. 94:8, R.C. editions=Ps. 95:8). And again. "He that
hath ears to hear, let him hear what the Spirit saith to
the Churches" (Rev. 2:7). "Come listen to me: I will
teach you the fear of the Lord". (Ps. 33:12, R.C. editions
=Ps. 34:11). "Run while you have the light of life, lest
the darkness overtake you" (John 12:35). That call to
awaken and to listen to the divine voice speaking to us
each day, was, of course, addressed to the sixth-century
monks of Monte Cassino, but relying heavily, as they do,
upon the Scriptures, they speak to a larger audience, that
is to all of us. "Today if you will hear his voice, harden
not your hearts." And God calls us through the voices of
the poor, of the hungry, of the oppressed; through the
anguish of the bereaved and the suffering; through the old
and the sick. "Harden not your hearts." To help and serve
these, in a special manner, is to help and serve Christ Himself, for He has told us that it is so (Mt. 25:40).

Jesus Christ, our way, our truth and life: it is in Him
that we shall discover the vision that gives meaning and
purpose to life. God did indeed speak to our fathers in
many ways and by many means, through the prophets;
"now at last in these times he has spoken to us with a
Son to speak for him ... a Son, who is the radiance of
his Father's splendour, and the full expression of his
being" (Hebrews 1:1–2). St Benedict, the teacher of the
monks, was only so because he was himself, first of all, a
disciple of Christ. His Rule gave to his monks and to
their sisters one way of living the Gospel. He outlined
principles, proposed a workable organisation for men or
women living in community, and he taught them a spiritual
doctrine according to which they could live and embark
upon that life-long search for God, which is the monk's
special task.

It is that spiritual doctrine – or at any rate one aspect
of it – which constitutes one answer to the question posed
at the beginning of this address: has St Benedict a message for the modern world?

The foolishness of man turned – as it always tends to
do – the garden of Eden into a jungle, a jungle of massive
power and beauty, but inhabited, alas, by suspicious and
fearful beings, who live, or are likely to do so, as rivals and
not as brothers and sisters; more affected by fear, than
inspired by love. But if we find the meaning and true
purpose of all things, and, most especially of man himself,
we shall have discovered the road that leads to good sense
and sanity. This is wisdom, the opposite of foolishness. It
is knowing, not only about things, but what they are for;
it is having a clear view of what has to be achieved, and
knowing what steps to take to attain it; it is not the
despising of human skill and success, but understanding
how to put these to good and beneficial use. St Benedict
called this "discretion, the mother of virtues". It is more
than knowledge, more subtle than skill. It enables us to see

life and ourselves, as God sees us; it makes us realise that we live in God's world, and not ours, that we are stewards and not proprietors; that others have rights, too, and all of us responsibilities to shoulder and duties to be undertaken. In short, we shall, with wisdom, discover that the two-fold command of the Gospel, to love God and our neighbour, should be at the very centre of our individual lives and inspire our relationships to one another. We shall have put on the mind of Christ.

St Benedict was a master of wisdom, not only because he had a clear vision of the purpose of human life, but because he also had a good understanding of human nature. He knew that we were wounded creatures, imperfect and foolish, but nevertheless immensely precious in the eyes of God. The garden will never be quite restored to what it was supposed to be, and the workmen in it will always be less than totally satisfactory. We are a fallen race. But the ideals are there, and unless we strive all the time to realise them we run the risk of being less than fully human. St Benedict teaches that the way to good sense and sanity will always be initially difficult, but if we persevere, we shall learn to move more quickly, and more sweetly.

Praise God, seek His will and do it, obey His commandments, in other words make certain that He comes first in our thinking and acting, and the rest will fall into place. "Seek ye first the Kingdom of God, and all things will be added to you." There is nothing original in all this, nothing new; it is ancient wisdom, and it is contemporary, for it is telling us how to be human, I mean fully human. Man without God is not. We need to know God, to love Him and to serve Him if we are to find happiness in this life as well as in the next, and to have purpose in all our undertakings. What is true for the individual is true also for every community, and so for that larger community which is today's society – the global village.

My brothers and sisters who follow the Rule of St Benedict, allow me, in all humility, I trust, to urge you to be faithful to that Rule and to the spirit of St Benedict. Just be yourselves, humbly confident of your heritage and aware of the part you must play in the life of the Church, which is the Body of Christ. We are part, and only part, of the great task of evangelisation which is so needed today. Our monasteries must witness to the values of the Kingdom of God, and as we do so we shall help to cultivate the garden in which is set the city of man. And to the dwellers within that city, St Benedict speaks too, saying to all of us: make God your first concern, live the Gospel, be faithful disciples of Christ, listen to the Spirit, and then we shall see our way to feeding the hungry, to helping the poor, to bringing peace to the world, to respecting life and nature. We shall know wisdom. Be sure of this: we shall not find the answers to the riddles of life other than in Christ, the wisdom of God. The vision is there; allow Him to touch our eyes, and we shall see it.

St John's Abbey, Collegeville, USA
20 June, 1980

I must confess that I do not normally instinctively turn to the book of Deuteronomy when I am in need of spiritual consolation. But some words from the first reading in today's liturgy came as a pleasant and unexpected surprise. I read: "Choose life so that you and your descendants may live in the love of Yahwe your God, obeying his voice, clinging to him, for in this your life consists" (Deut. 30:19, 20). As I read these words, and especially that part about "clinging to him, for in this your life consists", to my mind came back that verse from Psalm 119 (Ps. 118 R. C. editions):

Suscipe me, Domine, secundum
eloquium tuum et vivam, et
non confundas me ab expectatione mea

Receive me, Lord, in accordance with
your word and I shall live, and do not
let me be frustrated in my expectations.

What memories come back when we hear those words! How evocative they are, for they remind us of the youthful enthusiasm and generosity which was surely ours, when we promised before God and His saints, in the presence of the monastic community, to follow the Rule of St Benedict. "Receive me, Lord, accept me and I shall live, and that life consists in clinging to you." Surely we are right, as we celebrate this centenary year, to look back to the day of our Profession, and to try to recapture the wholehearted-ness and the generosity of that dedication of ourselves.

We may be older now, wiser perhaps and more experienced, and, no doubt, we have grown to realise that we have received more in our monastic lives than we have given. And, so I like to think, we begin to acknowledge that "our clinging to God" has become more simple, less complicated, but certainly stronger. No, we shall not be frustrated in our expectations. We shall live. Fidelity will be rewarded.

We do need to recapture the generosity and enthusiasm of our day of Profession. That is part of that personal renewal, which is prior to and fundamental for that general renewal of our monastic communities. The voice that called us years ago still calls us today. Every monastic day is a new monastic beginning. "If you obey the commandments of Yahwe your God", we heard in that same passage from the book of Deuteronomy, "and follow his ways, if you keep his commandments, his laws, his customs, you will live" (Deut. 30:16). There are echoes of this in the Prologue of the Rule, as you will recall. Not everything in the Prologue is immediately congenial and comfortable; but do not forget St Benedict's comments, where he says: "What can be sweeter to us, dearest brethren, than this voice of our Lord inviting us? Behold, in his loving mercy the Lord showeth us the way of life" (Prologue). Of course we have realised that the voice that is calling us, and bidding us to obey Him and follow His ways, does so, not because He has discovered that we want to "cling" to Him, but, quite the contrary, it is He who wants to cling to us. That is the reason why we always receive more in the monastery than we give.

It is all too easy to forget this desiring by God of us, or at least we can often fail to allow it to become real in our daily lives. Monks and sisters are busy people, and that is no bad thing, but from time to time, we have to hear the voice of the Lord saying to us: "Brother, or sister, you worry and fret about so many things and yet few are needed, indeed only one. It is Mary who has chosen the better part ..." (Lk. 10:41–42). That is the point: we have to know how to sit at the Lord's feet and listen to Him speaking. We always have to find space in the monastic day for that. It lies at the heart of personal renewal. The rest flows from it. Know how to "cling to him" in prayer, and then you will see the face of Christ more clearly in those whom you are called to serve. Was it the same Mary who had sat at His feet, and who later hurried off to busy herself with seeing what had happened to the body of the crucified Christ? She found Him in the garden, and clung to Him. When He called her name, she recognised Him.

Is it not that "clinging" to God, when heart speaks to heart *(cor ad cor loquitur)* that the change within us begins to take place; it is that change of heart which the Bible calls "metanoia", and which is the inner meaning of that vow, which we take, and is called *conversio morum*.

Our monastic life is, however, not simply the pursuit of an individualistic spirituality; it is more, and the model provided by the early Christians gives us a larger context and a deeper understanding of what our monasteries should be: "These remained faithful to the teaching of the apostles, to the brotherhood (and sisterhood), to the breaking of bread and to the prayers" (Acts 2:42). They lived in community, and so do we. It is the Christian instinct so to do.

St Benedict's own experience of the eremitical life must have taught him the advantage and the dangers of such a way. What the majority needed was life in the community, the *coenobium*. I have always thought that it is healthy if in a coenobite there be, from time to time, a yearning for the eremitical life. A successful community person is one who can enjoy solitude, and especially solitude spent with God. This claim may sound just a little pretentious; so I remind myself – and I can only speak for myself –

that somewhere in the depths of that unregenerated part of
me there lurks a potential "gyrovague", even, I must admit
it, a possible "sarabaite" – this latter expressing in one
word that desire or tendency to think, as the "sarabaites"
did, that "their law is their own good pleasure: whatever
they think of or choose to do, that they call holy; what
they like not, that they regard as unlawful" (R.B. Ch 1).
When the "gyrovague" or the "sarabaite" are strongest in
me, then I rejoice in the vow of stability. That vow roots
me in one particular monastic family. It is not a vow intended solely to protect me from my own wayward nature;
it reminds me that my search for God is done with others,
I helping them and they helping me. As a family, we live
in His name and for His purposes, so Christ is in our
midst. When we break bread together we are both expressing our unity and strengthening it.

The head of every monastery is Christ, but He needs a
visible representative, and that is why there are Abbots,
Abbesses and Prioresses. The Rule is bold, indeed shock-
ingly bold, when it states, in speaking of the Abbot; "he is
believed to be the representation of Christ in the monastery." This leads me to reflect for a moment on the value
of our vow of obedience. In recent years in religious life
there has tended to be a certain unease in respect of that
particular vow. We are unwise to belittle it. It needs faith,
and perhaps some years of monastic experience, to discover its value. It is one aspect of the monastic way which
ensures that our gift of ourselves is truly genuine, indeed
radical as well. It is my way of saying: I only want God,
and I want Him to do as He wills with me. More fundamen-
tally, it enables me to conform myself to a special characteristic of Christ's own life, which was His preoccupation
with the will of His Father. Ultimately, it is a sign of love.
Obedience is to be understood in the context of the language
of love. It is the outward sign of that inner total dedication
to another, of my desire to be for that Other; it is our gift

of ourselves and, paradoxically, it leads to our true freedom.

You will forgive me, I trust, for having concentrated on the vows in this celebration homily; the decision to do so arose in part from thoughts on our Scripture readings today. The idea of "clinging" to God as the way to the fullness of life in the monastic way, was particularly attractive, and it struck me that the vows were our God-given way of doing just that. Furthermore, it occurred to me to think that the most important thing that we could do to benefit from this centenary year was, in fact, to renew our Professions – to rededicate ourselves to our service of a loving Father. Such an act is, clearly, pleasing to God – "What can be sweeter to us, dearest sisters and brothers, than this voice of the Lord inviting us – behold in his loving mercy the Lord showing the way of life" (Prologue). Thank you St Benedict for saying that and much else.

Westminster Cathedral, London
11 July, 1980

You will recall the prophecy which St Benedict made about the future of his own monastery at Monte Cassino. St Gregory tells the story: "Almighty God has decreed" – so St Benedict said – "that this entire monastery and everything I have provided for the community shall fall into the hands of the barbarians." St Benedict is reputed to have said this "with many tears", not weeping as he usually did at prayer, but with deep sighs and lamentation." (Dialogues Ch 17). I have read that the sacking of Monte Cassino took place in the year 581 (McCann *St Benedict*); elsewhere I read that it was at some point between 581 and 589. In any case, the centenary we are celebrating in 1980 is due to be followed by a more sombre one, either next year, or in the years that follow ... because Monte Cassino was destroyed, and for years it lay in ruins.

Benedictinism, however, did not die with the collapse of monastic life at St Benedict's own monastery. The one single factor that ensured the continuation of all that St Benedict had achieved at Monte Cassino was, of course, the Rule. Monasteries throughout the centuries have come into being and then disappeared again – either destroyed from without by enemies, or disintegrated from within from lack of zeal and good observance – but the Rule remained.

Now the vandalism perpetrated against Monte Cassino by the Lombards had one important consequence which St Benedict had also foretold. None of the monks there lost their lives. They fled to Rome for refuge. Some people argue that this is why St Benedict's Rule became well known, both at the very centre of Western Christendom and also by one who was himself a monk and who was soon to be Pope: St Gregory the Great. The latter's influence was to be of particular importance. We who live in these parts have good reason to hold in special veneration St Gregory and his monastery on the Coelian Hill, since it was from there that St Augustine and his companions made their way to our shores in 597. Thus the influence of Roman monasticism, and, possibly, at least some knowledge of the Rule and of its author, came to Britain. Some years later, Benet Biscop and Wilfrid ensured that the Rule of St Benedict would prevail over all other Rules, and that the observance of Roman customs would end the Celtic monastic tradition, itself so rich and so much part of our ancient inheritance.

One might have expected after the Synod of Whitby in 664, that this island would have experienced a peaceful and gradual growth of monasticism. It was not to be. What had happened at Monte Cassino as a result of the Lombard attacks, happened here, too, in the wake of the Viking invasions. And this kind of thing was to happen again and again, notably and tragically in the sixteenth century. But the Rule itself was never lost. It remained the norm and the ideal. The ideal always needed to be rediscovered, and then monasticism in Britain experienced a new golden age.

One such golden age followed the reforms of Dunstan, Oswald and Ethelwold, in the tenth century; another, the influence of Cluny in the eleventh; and yet a third the all-important Cistercian movement of the twelfth. Then, too, I think of the revival of a vigorous monasticism at St Justina of Padua and of the Valladolid Congregation at the beginning of the seventeenth century, a revival which was rich in consequences for the refounding of the English Benedictine Congregation.

As far as I know, St Benedict made no other prophecy about his work except that Monte Cassino would be destroyed. But he must have known that monasticism itself would always endure. It had started two centuries before he himself was born in 480, and other monasteries existed in Western Europe during his lifetime. Why has it endured? Monasticism is very much part of the life of the Church. Indeed, it is a phenomenon found in many religions. Destroy it in one age, it will reappear in another; drive it out from one nation, it will take root elsewhere; if it dies in one place, it will be reborn somewhere else – with an almost stubborn persistence. Even today, monastic life fascinates some, intrigues others, puzzles and baffles. Sometimes it is misunderstood, even criticised, but often, happily, its very presence reassures and inspires other people. It is good to know that there are still men and women who are prepared to dedicate their lives to praising God and to labouring in His service without reward or credit in this life. Monks and nuns are not romantics; indeed they are generally pretty hardheaded. We know ourselves to be rather ordinary people, struggling to live up to an almost impossible ideal. We do our best, and that best is, more often than not, very good.

As we look back fifteen centuries and study the history of St Benedict and his Rule in our island, we thank God for this precious gift as we stand around this altar today. It is His Providence which has been at work since St Benedict's time, and if the contributions made by great abbeys and by individual monks and nuns to the life of the Church is for us a source of pride, we know that it is to God and not to ourselves that we must give the glory.

There are many of us, sons and daughters of St Benedict, gathered together in this cathedral today. We represent a great variety of ways of being "Benedictine". We have, each of us, been fashioned by the Rule of St Benedict, but our communities have had to respond down the ages to the different needs of the time. Is it not the case that, throughout our history, while the Rule has been our inspiration and provided the norms by which we live, the needs of the Church and of the times have determined our way of serving?

Bede was a scholar and devoted his life to that task, but there were hundreds of other monks at Wearmouth and Jarrow about whom we know nothing and who must have been engaged in very ordinary activities in that locality. Boniface is the prototype of the missionary monk. That particular service has ever been, and is to this day, part of our monastic heritage. Anselm represents a different role, that of an ecclesiastical dignitary concerned with the affairs of the state, as well as with those of the mind and the spirit. Ambrose Barlow, John Roberts and Alban Roe witnessed to the Gospels with their blood. Dame Gertrude More speaks of that life which is almost exclusively devoted to prayer. Aelred represents the power of a gentle and humane ruler, living in an austere situation. The contemplative, the scholar, the missionary, the martyr, the educator, the pastor – whether in diocese or parish – these are all part of our past, and they explain in large measure our present. We run schools, work in parishes, receive strangers into our midst, travel abroad to make foundations ... The list could go on. We can all think, too, of many other great names among the monks and nuns of the past, brilliant examples of the flexibility of the Rule and of the rich variety of its inspiration. But we must not forget those forefathers of ours, many of whom we ourselves have known and revered, men and women unknown, save to their own monastic communities and to a few friends. They are recalled to our minds each day when the Necrology is read. The unseen and unsung monks and nuns are the real treasures of the monastic life. Their value is known only to God, and it is, I would think, always better that way. It is God's judgment that we fear, not man's. It is God's praise that we covet, not the world's.

We are right to look back and to be grateful and, among friends, to rejoice that there have been fine periods in our history, and many holy monks and nuns in our monasteries. But we must not be complacent. Monte Cassino was destroyed soon after Saint Benedict's death, and it must surely have been a house of good observance. God's ways are not ours; His reasons and plans are often hidden from us.

We must think too, of the future and of our part in that. In this centenary year we shall be asking ourselves, as indeed others have been doing, what we can contribute to contemporary society. Others will ask us whether we are still relevant. What have we to say to the world in the 1980's? What are we doing about its problems? The questions are perfectly in order; though rarely easy to answer. Our world is indeed full of problems, and the signs of the times are clear: the dignity and rights of all men, women and children must be asserted and achieved; the hungry must be fed; peace between nations must be worked for; the environment protected; human life respected ... These are but some of the current issues. As monks and nuns, we cannot fail to be concerned with these matters. Indeed, not only our Christian teaching but our very humanity demands that we be sensitive to the needs of others, at least in the way we would wish them to be sensitive to ours. The Lord's command as recorded by St Matthew in his 25th chapter strengthens further the need for ordinary human compassion and for action to be undertaken. St Benedict was aware of this. In the chapter entitled, "The Tools of Good Works", he lists: relief of the poor, the clothing of the naked, the visiting of the sick, among those things which should concern the monk. No, we are not exempt from occupying ourselves with the social issues of our day. Perhaps even, at times, we may have to raise our voices about these things, when it is expedient to do so. On one famous occasion, St Benedict himself did just that. The Gothic king, Totila, was on his way through Campania to Naples, when he called at Monte Cassino. It was in the year 542. Saint Benedict issued a stern rebuke to the king: "You are doing much evil; cease now from your iniquity." Totila is said to have been less cruel after that.

Important though concern for the welfare of others may be, do not forget that for a monk and for a nun, concern for the social issues of the day is not sufficient. We must never cease, if we are to be true to ourselves and to St Benedict, to be preoccupied with the mystery of God and His love for all of us. Be convinced that there are many people in our day who wish to know about the real meaning and purpose of their lives and who are looking for a peace which cannot be attained, they are slowly discovering, outside the knowledge and recognition of God. Live the monastic life faithfully and lovingly, and you will have something precious to say and to show, which will encourage and enthuse visitors to your monasteries and to all those for whom you are in some manner responsible. Indeed, the seeking for God is always the search for relevance, for it is an entering into a world that is real, that is, a world understood as ultimately dependent upon God and answerable to Him for what it does, or does not.

The more we try to see the world as God sees it, the clearer will be our understanding of it, and the ways in which we can contribute to resolving its problems will be shown to us. There will be some moments when important decisions must be taken, when we shall have to answer a particular call from the Church, prompted by the Holy Spirit at work in the community. There will be many other moments when we shall need faith to see and understand that the model or prototype of monastic living is not only the early Christian communities, as described in the Acts of the Apostles, but also that hidden life of Jesus Christ at Nazareth. There was not much to show for those first thirty years, but were they not supremely precious in the eyes of the Father? Did they not, in ways we cannot measure, contribute to the welfare of a world which knew only contempt for the place chosen by the Lord for His home? The doing of ordinary things, day in and day out, out of love for God, is extraordinarily important. Our understanding of that, and our doing of it, can be a great encouragement and example to those thousands of persons whose lives are ordinary in the eyes of men, but are so valuable in the sight of God. This is the value of daily work.

Much emphasis has been laid in recent years, and rightly so, on the fact that the Christian response must be much concerned with the service of others. But to emphasise one value must not involve the denial of another. So may I be bold and exhort you, today's monks and nuns, to complement that emphasis: by asserting the value of that type of praying which has no other purpose than the delight of doing it for its own sake; by reminding the rest of us that the daily praising of God, the *opus Dei*, must have pride of place in the life of the Church, and that dignity and beauty in worship are values we cannot afford to lose; by continuing, especially, that exploration of the mystery which God is, which was so aptly summed up by St Benedict in the phrase: "the search for God". You know well that you cannot now see the fullness of the light, which will be the reward of all who are faithful, but you can catch a glimpse of that mystery as a gentle glow, a glow that already hints at the brilliance of the light that is at present hidden; but it is light, and it has warmth. It is of this mystery that you must speak to others, to help and to encourage. Many of you are much involved in pastoral and educational work, as I well know, and this is important, for you are well placed to give to others what, through living the Rule, you have received from God. What you have to give is much needed in our day. The present generation want to hear about God, and what they hear must have the ring of authenticity born of experience.

Today, the Church thanks you for what you have contributed for close on fifteen centuries as contemplatives, as educators, as mission priests, as scholars ...

And the Church awaits with holy eagerness for what you will give in the years to come. We know that it will be good.

Abbaye St Benoît-sur-Loire, France
13 July, 1980

It is always good to be with the monastic brethren, and especially in this year when we celebrate the fifteenth centenary of St Benedict's birth. For me there are personal and family reasons for wishing to be with the monks and nuns of France on this occasion, but these are not of the first importance. And I am happy, too, to be able to greet again monks whom I have been privileged to know from the days when we would meet at Sant' Anselmo for the Congress of Abbots. More importantly, it is a joy to be able to acknowledge the rich and varied contribution made by the monks and nuns of France to monasticism throughout history. It would take too much time to quote all the examples which come so easily to mind, but I am thinking, for instance, of the great learning which characterised the Congregation of St Maur in the seventeenth century, and of the work of Dom Guéranger in the nineteenth. Earlier still, the great reforms of Cluny and Citeaux originated in this part of the world. These and other influences, have affected the lives of many people outside France. My own country, in particular, owes much to your monastic forefathers. Anglo-Saxon monks who went on pilgrimage to the Eternal City, travelled through Gaul, where they halted and rested in your ancient abbeys before continuing their journeys refreshed and enriched by their new monastic experience. In the eleventh century, the Normans brought new vigour and life to English monasticism, and gave us some great Abbots, as well as those two famous monks, each of whom became Archbishop of Canterbury – Lanfranc and St Anselm. How much we owed to St Anselm, an Italian and

a former Prior of Bec, representing, as he does, the learning and sanctity of that great monastery, while Lanfranc
symbolises that gift for wise administration which is so
important a part of every monastery. And of course, I
cannot forget that my own monastic community spent
nearly two hundred years at Dieulonard, near Nancy, as
exiles from a hostile regime, until they were expelled from
your country in 1791.

Our purpose this year, is to recall the memory of St
Benedict, the Patriarch of the monks of the West. We are
to recapture his spirit, and we have to assess our contribution to the life of the Church. Our past achievements have
been important, for not only have Benedictines made
major contributions to the culture and civilisation of what
today we call Europe, but also, by our presence and witness, we have spoken to people of the things of God. And
we have spoken these things to other continents as well.
I do not forget that the organisation known as "l'aide pour
l'implantation monastique" is based upon French soil. In
our day, too, we must continue to be permanent reminders
to the men and women of our society that God has to be
at the very centre of all human and civilised living. We
shall do this if we remember always that our monasteries
must be, first of all, houses of prayer. We shall be true to
St Benedict if this be the case. What lay close to St Benedict's heart must also be close to ours.

The Rule, codifying ancient monastic experience and
wisdom, flexible and adaptable, humane and compassionate, has been and can continue to be, that instrument
which we may use to explore the mystery which God is.
Understand its fundamental principles, live by its spirit
and value its doctrine, and you will catch a glimpse of that
Glory of God which He accords from time to time to those
who strive, humbly and obediently to serve Him in the
schola servitii Domini.

I like to recall that vision which St Benedict had as he looked out from the tower, when he saw "the whole world as if gathered into one sunbeam". You will remember how St Gregory commented: *"animae videnti Creatorem angusta est omnis creatura"* – "to souls who see the Creator, all creation becomes small" (Dialogues Ch 35). If we but catch a glimpse of the glory of God, we see the world, its peoples and its events in their true perspective. We see them as they really are.

That vision which St Gregory describes is a summary, so I like to think, of the spirituality of St Benedict. He has a strong sense of what it means to be Creator, and he seems to have discovered the meaning of the phrase "the glory of God". Before the Creator, man is small, and he must recognise his dependence and acknowledge the demands which God's will makes upon him. Hence the stress which St Benedict puts upon humility as a fundamental monastic virtue and upon obedience as a certain way for the monk to conform to the will of God. In prayer there must be reverence, and we have to consider "how we ought to behave in the presence of God and his angels, and so sing the psalms that mind and voice may be in harmony" (R.B. Ch 19). The humble man acknowledges the greatness and the majesty of God. Obedience can appear to be an uncongenial and burdensome principle by which to live, until the monk learns that it is the love of God for him which must be the all-embracing motive that determines his thinking and acting. That love of God which is warm, strong and intimate, and which includes His power, mercy and beauty, is the "glory of God". We discover this "glory" gradually, over the years, perhaps after periods of darkness and doubt, but "as we progress in our monastic life and in faith, our hearts shall be enlarged and we shall run with unspeakable sweetness of love in the way of God's commandments". This is the re-

ward for fidelity and perseverance; it is the gift that comes
with the victory over our restless natures by our vow of
stability.

These reflections on the majesty of our Creator and on
that glory of God of which the Scriptures speak, explain
the central part which the praise of God played in the
life of St Benedict, and so must play in our lives, too. The
opus Dei, to which nothing must be preferred, remains
today, as it has been in the past, the most important
activity of the monastic day. It does not matter, to my
mind at any rate, whether we sing in Latin or in the
vernacular, but it does matter that our worship be done
with dignity and reverence – *digne, attente ac devote*. We
are right to enjoy the intimacy of a loving Father; wrong
to forget that we must also bow down and acknowledge
our littleness before our Lord and Creator.

Where did St Benedict first begin to explore the mystery
of God? Perhaps he had gone in search of Him to the
schools of Rome, but he did not find Him there. He saw
corruption around him, and so he left Rome, "knowingly
ignorant and wisely unlearned". Nor was he satisfied with
his stay among the Christians at Enfide. Here he met with
praise and adulation, and these are enemies as dangerous
as moral corruption. He would seek God in solitude and
silence in the cave at Subiaco. Much later on he was to
speak of heavenly things with Scholastica, and with many
others who came to learn from his wisdom and experience.
But all of this was only possible because he had read and
reflected upon the word of God, and had met in prayer that
Word "who is the radiance of his Father's splendour and
the full expression of his being" (Heb. 1:3). How much
our modern world needs to learn the values of silence and
solitude which provide the context in which to pursue that
meditation on divine things which we call *lectio divina*.

Of course, like St Benedict, we have in our own time
discovered the value of community. St Benedict knew from

experience that it was good to be silent and alone, but forced, as he was, to abandon the eremitical life, he grew to appreciate the riches that are to be found within a community of "one heart and of one mind". After all, his Rule is meant "to provide for the strong race of cenobites". The scriptural basis for life in community was clear: "They persevered with one accord, day by day, in the Temple worship, and, as they broke bread in this house or that, took their share of food with gladness and simplicity of heart, praising God, and winning favour with all the people" (Acts 2:46). That description of life in the early Christian community has been, for many commentators on the monastic life, the prototype of life in the monastery. This is not surprising, for the Rule of St Benedict is presented to us as one way of living out our baptismal vows and of following the Gospel.

So, silence and solitude must be part of the monk's spirituality; they are essentially inner dispositions, coexisting with external activity and the burdens of responsibility for others, moments of desert experience in a busy day, but also making important contributions to community life. We need to share silence with God to be able to share spiritual riches in community; we must love solitude to be able to contribute to life in community.

Monks, wherever they live, must, like the early Christian communities, "win favour with all the people". We do not as monks, exist only for ourselves. We have a long and noble tradition of receiving guests into our midst, and they are to be received as Christ Himself. Today, people are looking for and seeking access to the spiritual riches which we should have discovered and which ought to be made available to them in our monasteries. Then, too, Benedictines in the past have been much involved with direct missionary work. I think of Augustine coming to England; of Boniface going to Germany; of Anskar in Scandinavia and of Adalbert's mission to the Slavs ... St Benedict him-

self preached to those who lived near the monastery. We
are part of the Church. Christ's Church – as the Second
Vatican Council reminded us – is missionary, pilgrim, pastoral, and evangelising by nature. Our love of Christ, then,
will involve us in a variety of pastoral activity at different
times. In thinking about this, I recall a saying of St
Thomas: *"sicut enim maius est illuminare quam lucere
solum, ita magis est contemplata aliis tradere quam solum
contemplari"* (II II 188 a.b.) – "as it is a greater thing to
illuminate than just to shine; so it is a greater thing to pass
on to others those things which have been contemplated,
than just to contemplate."

Rejoice, dear brothers and sisters, in this centenary year.
Have confidence and hope. Our Benedictine life is good in
itself and it has much to offer to men and women today.
What it has achieved in the past in helping to establish the
kingdom of God in the world, it will continue to do in the
future. And we shall all have reason to be grateful again
for the special gifts which you can offer.

Church of St Begh, Whitehaven, West Cumbria
27 July, 1980

For just over a hundred years, the parishes of West Cumbria were served by the sons of St Benedict, so it is very right that today you should be celebrating the fifteenth centenary of St Benedict's birth. Many of you have personal and affectionate memories of Benedictine priests who spent the greater part of their lives in your midst; just as the towns of West Cumbria are familiar names in our monasteries. Indeed, they have been in our prayers for a long time, going right back to the eighteenth century when our fathers were still exiles abroad.

Times change, and the monasteries have not been able to continue their parish apostolate to you on the same scale as formerly. What concerns us above all, however, is that you should continue to have priests, and it is a joy for us, the monks, to know that priests from the Lancaster diocese now serve you with the same devotion and care. It is the priest who matters; he is the one who brings the Mass to you, who cares for you and brings you God's grace at crucial and important moments in your lives. Thank God for your priests, and we, the monks, thank Him in particular, today, that our Benedictine fathers are still among you in West Cumbria.

There have been many celebrations all over the world this year in honour of St Benedict. We have been recognising, fifteen hundred years after his birth, just how important his life and work have been for the Church. Although he lived so long ago, we know something about him from the writings of St Gregory the Great, the Pope who sent the monk St Augustine to evangelise our country in the

year 597. We can also deduce quite a lot about Saint
Benedict from the Rule he wrote for his monks, because
St Gregory tells us that he lived what he wrote. The Rule
puts before monks and nuns a high ideal of the way to be
a Christian, and St Benedict lived that ideal. From the
Rule we can see that St Benedict was a wise man, compassionate and full of zeal for the glory of God.

Today, people are asking whether St Benedict has any
special message for us who live in the twentieth century.
After all he lived fifteen centuries ago, and much has happened and changed since then. That, of course, is un-
doubtedly true, but there are some things that do not
change and among these are the fundamental principles of
the spiritual life. I am going to speak about these because
I believe that in the Church of today, that is in the Church
of the Second Vatican Council, we have not really understood what Pope John XXIII and Pope Paul VI intended
when they called us to "renewal". What they meant was
that the Church's response to the needs of the contemporary world depends ultimately on each one of us. It is the
deepening of our own personal spiritual lives that is essential if the Church is to play her proper part in today's
world. Hence, they asked us to change ourselves so that
we could help to change the world into a happier and a
better place. But such a change in us is only possible if we
turn to God and recognise that Jesus Christ is our way to
the Father. He came to tell us the truth about God and to
give us a new life, a life of intimacy with Him, where His
love would fulfil our longing and our desire for Him.

Now St Benedict also spoke of these things and what he
wrote can still help us today. What he says does not just
concern monks and nuns; it concerns you as well. St Benedict was a master of spiritual things. He knew his craft.
Those who came to his monastery at Monte Cassino came
to learn. In fact he called the monastery a "school of the
service of the Lord". I like to call that school, in which a

monk learns how to love God, a "school of love". The reason is clear: at the heart of the Gospel, that good news given to you and to me, is the twofold commandment to love God and to love our neighbour. We do not automatically love God and our neighbour in the way that Our Lord means us to love them. This love has to be learnt and practised. It takes time and effort. The monastery is a school for learning such love. But the monastery is not only a school; it is also a family. Monks are brothers; nuns are sisters; and the Abbot who rules the monastery, is so-called because the title "abbot" means "father".

So the monastery is a family, and a family of persons learning how to serve God, which means loving Him. But to have said that, is to have described, too, what every ordinary family should be, namely a "school of the Lord's service", or, as I prefer to call it, a "school of love". It is in our own family that we first learn what love means. When we have begun to understand what human love is, then we begin to realise what love must be like in God – so much greater, warmer, stronger and more intimate than any way we can love each other. That is one reason why a stable and happy home is so important. It provides parents and children with the right environment in which to learn about the love of God. And once we begin to discover that, then we want to know more about God, and the more we know Him, the more we want to give Him loving service.

You might now be saying to yourselves: "Well, I suppose I should have gone to a monastery to find all this out." Not at all. God calls some people to the monastery to serve Him in this particular way; but most Christians remain, as we say, "in the world". They get married, have a family, go to work, and get involved in social life. There are many different "vocations" but each one is a call from God. St Benedict would say to you: "No, you are not meant to be a monk; but in my Rule you will find age-old principles which you can make your own, and which can

help you to realise that your life – all that you do and all
that happens to you – is your service of God."

If you ask a monk what he does in the monastery, he will
probably give you a long list of different jobs which fill up
most of his day. There are, however, three groups or cat-
egories into which everything else fits. These are : prayer,
reading and studying, and work. To learn to love God, we
have to do each of these three things : we have to pray;
we have to read about and think about God; and we have
to see our work as our way of serving Him. In the monastery we do all these things as members of a monastic
family. Those who are not monks must do them in their
own families first, and also in the parish family – for the
parish is a family, too.

Let us think about work first. By work I mean the
activities of each day, either carried on outside the home
in our place of employment, or done at home. Even when,
sadly, there is no work available for us – and what a
tragedy that is – nevertheless there are still things that we
do, either to improve the home, or just to keep ourselves
busy. We need to understand that everything we do is
precious in the eyes of God, that is everything except sin.
All that Our Lord did at Nazareth, in what we call His
hidden life, pleased and delighted His Father. Why? Because Our Lord loved His Father. It was not so much
what He actually did, but the loving heart with which He
did it that mattered. So it is with us : if we are trying to
love God, then all that we do pleases our Father. Everything becomes an act of love.

How do we try to love God? Where do we start? This is
the importance of prayer. Prayer is many things, but it is
always an attempt to reach out beyond ourselves to God –
or we can think of it as entering into ourselves to find Him
in the deepest depths of ourselves. Have you not known
yourselves, moments of great joy and peace, when you have
almost had a foretaste of the kind of happiness which

shall be ours one day? Have you not experienced, also, moments of great sadness, near despair, perhaps, when your whole self has seemed to cry out for some great love to come to you, to envelop you and bring you peace again? Such stirrings in our depths are constant appeals to God to listen to us and to be with us. St Benedict calls it "searching for God". In his monastery the monks were to be at prayer regularly each day – on some days this would be a delight; on others, a burden. But the lesson he taught is clear: we need regularity and discipline to keep at it. And that is one of his messages to you. Find time in the day which you can, so to speak, waste with God; make it regular, and be faithful to it, however short it is and no matter how you are feeling. When prayer is not easy, and we do it nonetheless, we are proving that we are trying to love God. And if you stick at it, God will begin to speak to you – for, as you well know, it is He who is in fact in search of us. He wants us, and always more than we can ever want Him.

We should, too, learn all we can about God. Get to know Our Lord, for He is God who became one of us, and He shows us what God is like. All His words and all His actions are so precious. Listen to His words in the Scriptures when you hear Mass, and think about what you have heard. Re-read those words on your own, and discuss them in groups in your own homes. This kind of activity will help you to pray, and as you pray more and better, you will become more aware of the presence of God in your lives.

Many people today are wanting the world to make sense for them; they want reassurance that there is a God, who is interested in them, cares for them, indeed, loves them. You who know Jesus Christ have to give Him to others – by your example, by your calm convictions and by the way you are concerned for other people. St Benedict gives us one particular means of becoming true followers of Christ –

it is by starting again on each new day to work away at it in the school of the Lord's service which is the school of love.

Abbey of St Scholastica, Subiaco, Italy
28 September, 1980

I doubt whether there have been many occasions in history
when representatives of nearly all the Conferences of
Bishops of Europe have made a pilgrimage together. This
is an important moment, and the timing and circumstances
of it are significant too. We are praying together at a time
when the Synod of Bishops is about to commence its work
on one of the most vital issues of our time, namely "the
role of the Family in the Modern World". Indeed it is the
presence of bishops of other continents in Rome for the
Synod which has made it possible for so many of them to
join us today and to pray with us for the needs of the
Church in Europe. The interests and concerns of the
bishops of one continent are shared today, and indeed
always, by the bishops of other lands. We the bishops of
Europe are one with our brethren in what concerns them.
Such mutual collaboration, expressing the idea of the co-
responsibility of the whole College of Bishops for the life
of the Church in every part of the world, is one of the main
characteristics of the ecclesiology of the Second Vatican
Council. On this day, too, the Council of the Conference of
European bishops is to issue a statement which is a call
to our fellow Christians and to others to shoulder our
responsibilities within Europe both today and tomorrow.
We are asking that all should work to establish justice and
peace among and within the nations of our continent, and
we are urging all to engage in the great work of evangelisation, to which the Second Vatican Council and the Synod
of Bishops of 1974 have called us. We have chosen to make
our pilgrimage to Subiaco and to issue our statement here,

for we are celebrating the fifteenth centenary of the birth
of St Benedict. The fact that Pope Paul VI proclaimed St
Benedict Patron of Europe makes our pilgrimage and our
prayer at Subiaco all the more appropriate.

It may be thought that this pilgrimage of European
bishops to Subiaco is a journey into the past, a nostalgic
commemoration of ancient values and former glories that
are now the fading religious and cultural heritage of by-
gone days. This is not so. Of course, it is our intention to
give thanks to God for the graces given through St Benedict, the Patriarch of Western Monasticism, and they have
been many; but our intention is also to find strength and
inspiration for the pilgrim Church in Europe as she makes
her way in this last quarter of the twentieth century. St
Benedict, like all great saints of every age and culture, can
still speak to us today, for his life and teaching are an
illustration and an expression of the principles and doctrines of the Gospel of Jesus Christ. There are, as we all
know, ancient spiritual values of fundamental importance
which are always new and always contemporary in any age.
It is upon these that we have come to reflect in this holy
place.

We recall first of all that it was to Subiaco that St
Benedict came as he turned his back on the corruption
which he had seen in Rome. He was a young man in
search of God; it was in silence and solitude that he set
out to hear the voice of God, and to enjoy the companion-
ship of Him alone. *"Solus in superni spectatoris oculis
habitavit secum,"* wrote St Gregory (Dialogues Bk II, 3)
which was the writer's manner of saying that the saint
lived now alone in the presence of God. Benedict was
hidden from men, observed only by God. That scrutiny by
God is demanding, and painful often, for when God wishes
to possess a person totally, there will be trials and tribula-
tions. St Gregory records some of the difficulties experienced by Benedict; he had to pass through the narrow gate

that leads to a new vision of life and a deeper understanding of the Gospel. So it will be for us too from time to time.

Did St Benedict, the hermit, hope and expect to live and die in the austerity of his cave amidst the wild beauty of this valley? We do not know. In fact he was called away from the eremitical life to become involved with other people. The monks of a neighbouring monastery – tradition says at Vicovaro – asked Benedict to be their Abbot. It did not work. The standards of the new Abbot were too high for the community, and Benedict's discipline too strict. The monks decided to get rid of their Abbot. They poisoned his wine. But the Abbot's blessing smashed the cup as if it had been struck by a stone. He was saved, but the monks lost their Abbot.

Wine is good, unless it be used for ignoble purposes or it be mixed with noxious ingredients. It is thus always with the gifts of God. If we use His gifts without acknowledging from whom they come, or use them for purposes which are different from His, then the good wine of man's achievements becomes sour and, worse still, can poison our lives. It can be thus in our society today: our scientific and technological achievements are rightful objects of our pride, and especially when we use our God-given skills to share in God's creative power and so write yet another new hymn of praise to the Glory of God. But if we ignore this vision of what should be and misuse our talents, then what should be wine to cheer the hearts of men becomes poison with a terrible power to kill. Think of how we have, in our day, constructed frightening weapons of destruction. Think, too, how a frenzied desire for material goods can poison the spirit of man, and lead to rivalries, dissensions and neglect of the poor and the needy. St Benedict reminds us that in all things God must be glorified; that is a fundamental principle. If we reject God and overthrow the standards demanded by the Gospel, then we have no ultimate purpose by which to live. We sink into the absurd.

To be in search of meaning and purpose in life is to seek
God, and that search is, for most of us, to be done by
collaboration and mutual assistance. No community can
survive for long and succeed, unless Christ be at its head,
for it is then that there is a proper hierarchy of values. We
may continue to reflect further upon these things in the
light of St Benedict's experience, and consider his second
attempt to build up a true Christian community. The twelve
small monasteries of Subiaco, under the direction of their
Abbot, did succeed. Perhaps St Benedict had learned at
Vicovaro, that the bruised reeds must not be broken, that
persuasion, understanding and compassion are essential
tools for every ruler. There must be principles, clear and
firm, of course, but the spiritual ruler's role is to enable
Christ to be and to live within those whom the leader is
called to serve, rather than to lay burdens upon their backs.
Such was St Benedict's approach, and his monks responded
to him. But he could not remain at Subiaco.

St Benedict was driven away by a jealous and turbulent
priest, called Florentius. This priest used a symbol of friendship, blessed bread, to be a minister of death. It was
poisoned. Again St Benedict escaped death. This having
failed, Florentius tried to corrupt the monks by exposing
them to temptation. St Benedict, realising that he was the
object of all this hatred, decided to leave Subiaco, and so
the great monastery of Monte Cassino was founded. Thus
he who had been teaching the manner of living in community in accordance with his Master's precept to live by
love, himself became the victim of hatred and dissension.
And may we not reflect that almost two thousand years
after the Lord had commanded us to live as brothers and
sisters in Christ, we can still make each other the victims
of cruelty and violence; still neglect each other in our
needs, allowing one part of the world to grow rich while
another starves to death; still refusing to give to all people

the respect and freedom which is theirs by right as sons and daughters of a loving Father.

We do right when we speak out in defence of persons. Society exists for their welfare, and not the other way round. But more is needed than condemnation of evils. We have to give the good wine of the Gospel to all men and women; we must tell them about Him who said, "I am the bread of life ... the bread which comes down from heaven is such that he who eats it never dies" (John 6:48–49). And there is that other bread and that other wine which play a special part in the life of the Christian community. Bread and wine are never put to so noble a use as when that bread becomes His Body and the wine His Blood in that great act which is the Eucharist, sign and cause of our one-ness in Christ and of the divine life which is His most precious gift. The poisoned bread and wine offered to Benedict were counter-signs of that unity and life which are the essence of the Christian community.

The Eucharist must once again become Europe's greatest treasure, and as in the past, the skill of the architect and of the musician will surround it with that dignity and beauty which is right when we handle so great a mystery on solemn occasions. The Gospel must be heard again and commend itself not only to those who have never heard it before, but to those, too, who have, alas, forgotten or re-jected it.

Now I believe that many men and women in our Western society are hungry and thirsty for values that will give meaning to their lives and purpose to their activities. These, unknowingly and unacknowledged, are in need of God. This should not be surprising, for there is in the human person a void which only the love of God can fill. And Europe itself is in search of its soul, and that soul will only be found when the void is filled by the Gospel in all its simplicity and purity. People are looking for spiritual leaders whose message is at once convincing, relevant and

satisfying. They are hungry for truth. The responsibility
that rests upon us, the Ministers of the Gospel, is very
great, but we think of it as our privilege rather than as our
burden.

Our manner of presenting the Gospel has to be positive
and encouraging. We must be listeners, too, as well as
preachers; indeed no one can preach wisely and to good
effect unless he listens to the real needs of the people. Compassion and understanding will enable us to appreciate the
difficulties of good people struggling to serve Christ in an
immensely complex and complicated world. For my part I
never cease to wonder at the frailty of human nature which
is our common lot, and at the same time to marvel at the
great destiny to which we are called by Jesus Christ. It is
like the striking contrast between the high hills that surround us here and the depths of the valleys below them.
Life is a pilgrimage out of the valley of man's depressed
state to the heights of the hills where, as was the case with
Moses, the glory of God can be seen. Bishops, with their
priests, are spiritual leaders on that journey. St Benedict
can advise us on how we should be, for he has much to
say on spiritual leadership. This sixth-century wisdom is,
surprisingly and happily, very contemporary. Allow me,
then, to leave the final word to St Benedict, as he speaks of
the Abbot of the monastery. This passage is always an
admirable examination of conscience; "Let him study
rather to be loved than to be feared. Let him not be turbulent or anxious, overbearing or obstinate, jealous or too
suspicious, for otherwise he will never be at rest. Let him
be prudent and considerate in all his commands; and
whether the work which he enjoins concern God or the
world, let him always be discreet and moderate, bearing
in mind the discretion of holy Jacob, who said: 'If I cause
my flock to be overdriven, they will all perish in one day.'
So, imitating these and other examples of discretion, the

mother of the virtues, let him so temper all things that the strong may still have something to long after, and the weak may not draw back in alarm." (R.B. Ch 64).

Epilogue

The journeys undertaken in praise of Benedict are now completed; a filial duty has been discharged. The thoughts contained in these homilies and addresses do not add to our knowledge of the Saint, nor do they claim to present a new understanding of his significance as a historical personage. They have been just one of several contributions made during this year of celebration. The opportunity to think further about the Rule and about the stories told by St Gregory has been one advantage; the journey of exploration into St Benedict's mind has been another.

What was St Benedict really like? What was the secret of his holiness? His Rule, as St Gregory tells us, is, in a sense, autobiographical; it can tell us much about St Benedict's spirituality. "He wrote a Rule for monks that is remarkable for its discretion and its clarity of language," St Gregory writes. "Anyone who wishes to know more about his life and character can discover in his Rule exactly what he was like as an Abbot, for his life could not have differed from his teaching" (Dialogues Bk II, 36). We think of St Benedict, then, as the ideal monk, as one, therefore, who lived as the Rule prescribes, and by this means discovered all the riches and excitement known to those who have penetrated to the heart of the Gospel message, that is to a true understanding of the meaning of what it is to love God, and our neighbour as ourselves.

The great Saints understand this in ways hidden from the rest of us. But what is possible for them is, indeed, with God's grace, possible for us. We do well to remind ourselves that the exploration of the mystery which God is, does from time to time lead us on a journey through darkness. It would be foolish, and wrong, to omit to say that. Sometimes the way is painful, sometimes the difficulties we face appear insuperable. We need tenacity and courage. There are hints, both in the Rule and in the writings of St Gregory, that St Benedict knew these things. He stuck at it, and he seems to have achieved a peace and a serenity that comes only as gift from God. It will be so for us if we, too, stick at it. It would be quite wrong, however, to think of our own voyages of discovery as being through unending darkness and ever painful. It is not so. There are often moments of light and times when the going is good. We have to be reflective in a world that makes reflection difficult. We need to find "space" in busy lives, to savour the good times, and "space" too, to understand, and accept, when the call is to tread after the Master over the hill that is called Calvary. It is indeed a privilege to be beckoned to follow that road; although it is not always easy to appreciate that. But it does lead eventually to the experience of new life, "a life hidden away now with Christ in God" (Col. 3:3), for we are risen with Christ, and our thoughts go beyond what we can see, hear and touch, to realities which lie beyond the senses. It is the Easter experience, and the prelude to that is to have known the desolation of Good Friday.

Now St Benedict gathered ordinary people around him. Men and women came together in community and followed his Rule in their own monasteries as they still do today. He gave them a new way of looking at life, precisely because they were to learn to put God at the very centre of their lives. That is the key for all of us. Once that starts to happen, then we begin to listen to the voice of God, which speaks in so many different ways, but pre-eminently in that Word of God which is the New Testament. We then see things differently. We find meaning and purpose to our own lives; we are slowly discovering reality. The preoccupations of secular man, important and vital though these may be, are no longer our sole preoccupations. We want to do other things. We need to react to whatever glimpses of His "glory" have been given to us, and praise becomes an important part of our offering; times of solitude along with God are golden moments snatched from a busy schedule with compelling insistence; reading the Scriptures and learning from the masters of the spiritual life are seen as enrichments; the help and support of groups with the same ideals and preoccupations are sought; work becomes a loving service, and the needs of our neighbours a prime concern.

The programme for monks and nuns is clear. The Rule is their guide. They have their way 'to which God has called them. That is their vocation. But St Benedict does speak, also, to those outside the monastic life. It would seem odd – or at least it would seem so to me – if people who must go to work each day and must care for families cannot, through these activities, achieve a high degree of holiness and be very close to God. If it is not possible, then the hidden life of Our Lord at Nazareth would make little sense, and the values and precepts of the Gospel would be meaningless. It cannot be. Once God is put at the centre of a life, then the rest follows. There are not higher and lower grades among Christians, as if one way of life were superior to another or inferior. There are different vocations. Holiness is offered to each of the baptised. Fidelity to duties and responsibilities in whatever walk of life, a desire to draw closer to God, service generously given to others, and especially to those in special need, these are certain signs that we are on the right road. The fundamental principles of the spiritual life are the same for all; the working out of these principles differs in accordance with varying circumstances. But for many people living and working in the ordinary circumstances of a normal everyday life, raising the mind and heart to God is often not easy. It is trying that matters. "Trying" is our part; whatever success we achieve is a gift from God. But it is sad when a person becomes convinced that following an ordinary career precludes that person from being close to God. It is often not a question of changing our style or the externals of life (although there are, of course, situations where this may be necessary), but rather a change in ourselves that is required. And we need an incentive to make the change; by far the most attractive of these is the desire to explore the meaning of God's great love for each one of us, a love which is at once warm, intimate and powerful. That thought should begin to dominate our prayer-life.

What lies at the heart of monastic spirituality can speak to us all. It is timeless, and so always relevant. There are other ways, of course. St Benedict has no monopoly. It is the Gospel that matters, and the various masters of the spiritual life do no more than show how the Gospel can be lived. So St Benedict points to the Master of all spiritual matters, that is to Our Lord Jesus Christ, and that is clearly most important. Our journey of exploration into the mystery which God is has to be done with Our Lord. He shows us the way. Indeed it is more than this, for He shares His life with us as our lives become increasingly involved with Him. The Father and He send the Holy Spirit to us to give light to our minds and warmth to our hearts. We must want that light and warmth, and ask for them. They are gifts.

So whether we live in monasteries or not, there is something always new to be learned from St Benedict. We have had his Rule for close on fifteen centuries. It can still inspire and help. To have discovered that again has been one of many blessings during this year of celebration. St Benedict's sons and daughters have every reason to be grateful, and it will be good if they continue to put before

us all a spirituality that is both sane and human. After all –
we are only completely human beings when we put God at
the centre of our individual lives, and offer Him our praise
and service. We are made for that.